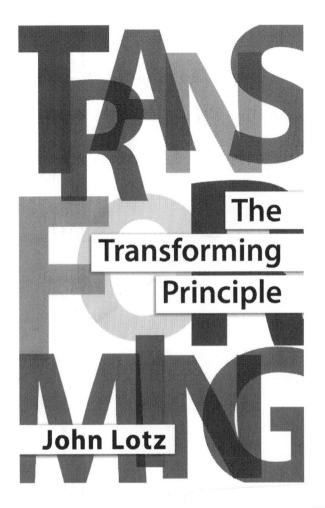

The
Transforming
Principle

John Lotz

malcolm down

PUBLISHING

First published 2023 by Malcolm Down Publishing Ltd.
www.malcolmdown.co.uk

27 26 25 24 23   7 6 5 4 3 2 1

British Library Cataloguing in Publication Data
A catalogue record for this book is available from the British Library.

ISBN 978-1-915046-59-8

Cover design by Angela Selfe
Art direction by Sarah Grace

Printed in the UK

Contents

Foreword

There is theory and there is practice; there is teaching and there is doing; there is the Bible and there is everyday life. Often these pairs are stretched far apart, or not even connected, and this is especially true when it comes to how we follow Jesus' inspirational teaching and then attempt to put it into practice. Moreover, it is acutely true when it comes to Jesus' words on generosity, giving and how we handle our resources and finances.

John has a rare gift of being a theorist and a practitioner. Perhaps this is due to his many years' experience in the medical profession as a surgeon and a medical director in our County Hospital, in Stafford. From student, to junior doctor, to registrar, to consultant, all that John has learned and carried on learning in his profession, he put into practice – it was fact it was the practise of his work that enabled him to grow in expertise, confidence and success.

In the same way John practises what he preaches in this book. John has taken what looks like a good but counterintuitive and perhaps impossible teaching on giving by Jesus and decided to live it out. In that way John is a true disciple – a learner and doer. It is the exciting inspiration of Jesus that has gripped his life and given him the faith to become a generous and joyful giver himself.

As well as being a medical doctor, John is a Bible teacher. He loves the Bible and he loves to engage with it – the tricky bits included – and then explains his findings to others. So, this is both a handbook of personal experience and a well-researched commentary on how to live in the God-given realty, that it is truly 'more blessed to give than to receive'.[1] I encourage you to learn from it and also to open your heart, as you read the personal testimony that pours off its pages.

There used to be a hand-drawn cartoon of a stick-figure surgeon in the foyer of our church building, that said 'Lotzy will get you in the end' – prophetic graffiti of fear, respect and trust! This book is John's personal offering of life, learning and experience to us and if we read it with open hearts and minds, Lotzy will get us in the end! Or more truly, the blessing of God's generous way of life will heal us and renew us; the scalpel of the words of Jesus will bring us into abundant life, like they have for John.

Martin Young
Former senior leader Rising Brook Baptist Church, Stafford

---

1. Acts 20:35.

Introduction

St Paul, in Philippians 3:12-14, describes his life as like a race. This is not about 'scoring points' or 'coming first', but completing the course – therefore we can all 'win'. Different gifts, abilities, limitations, opportunities and ages are not a handicap. They offer right variations in the course – we are not competing against each other. Therefore, we can encourage each other as we run together, and all celebrate at the end. The finishing point is the same for all.

How we run is the subject of this book. Attitude is vital. That means commitment, spirit, drive and clear decisions about what is not just 'important', but what is 'essential' in our expression of the Christian life. This is not about grim determination; God intends us to enjoy these experiences. Joy is an important Bible word!

So often, in the course of 'normal' Christian living (which includes Bible reading and praying, and attending church), something important 'hits you in the eye' – maybe a Bible passage, phrase, or even a word. You may have read it many times before, but never noticed it, then suddenly . . . I can think of several, but the subject of this book *The Transforming Principle*, 'It is more blessed to give than to receive', found in Acts 20:35, has stuck with me ever since I first saw it in 1976; something simple, but profound, unspectacular, but always relevant.

It is so central in the Bible that you can miss it! It marks all the great characters, Paul (who quoted it), being one, but Jesus (who said it) was the greatest of all. Throughout history, it has led people (often 'unlikely' people) into significant achievements, sometimes at great personal cost. It is at the heart of 'mission' – overseas and at home, and also in the life of often-unseen workers in local churches. You do not have to be 'famous' to be great!

My approach to the subject is often interrogative, to engage and stimulate the reader to think and if necessary, to act. There are many biblical references, mainly from the NIV 2011 version. Chapter 2 is essentially a Bible study.

The 'Transforming Principle' is a stimulus to the continuing discovery of possibilities and opportunities to invest into what God is saying. When He speaks, the only appropriate answer is 'yes'! And that is where the giving comes in – not loss, but investment! This has led me into many unexpected situations – some exciting, some unpleasant, some personally challenging – and out of them, onwards into more! Christian faith is not static; it either moves forwards or slows down, becomes stagnant and then slips backward. Its main limitation is disobedience to what God is saying. That may come through fear, pretending that it is not really God ('just my imagination'), or wrong priorities, which may even appear 'spiritual'. The outcome will always be disappointment, disillusionment and dissatisfaction; missing out on what could have been and should have been – achievement, encouragement and excitement.

True Christianity is dynamic and alive, indeed it *is* Life!

Chapter 1

A Shocking Truth

St Paul had a very soft spot for Ephesus. His first visit there was a stop-off on the way home from Corinth to Syrian Antioch, his mission-sending Church.[2] He was probably eyeing up the city, realising it was a very important centre commercially and strategically, thus ripe for preaching the gospel locally, to reach into the whole region. This proved to be correct, as evidenced by the letters to the seven churches in the book of Revelation, and Paul's own letters. Today, even in ruin, it is evident that this was a very large and significant city. It had an important harbour and spectacular public buildings, including a huge theatre. Most of the city has still not been excavated. There was interest in what Paul was teaching, followed by a request to stay. He left his two colleagues, Priscilla and Aquila, there to continue where he had left off and promised to return.

His next journey there took him on foot through Asia Minor and when he arrived in Ephesus, there was clear evidence that Christian ministry had moved on.[3] There were already twelve men who were 'disciples' but needed to expand their understanding of the Faith, through baptism and then receiving the Holy Spirit. It was now time

---

2. Acts 18:18-22.
3. Acts 19:1-7.

to stay with them, and he then moved into his usual pattern of ministry, starting with his own (Jewish) people in their synagogue. Three months debating with them eventually produced rejection and a parting of their ways. Not to be put off, he hired a public hall to continue his work. Many people came to faith, miracles happened and demons were driven out. The reality of their faith was evidenced by public confession and practical repentance. The gospel changes thinking and then behaviour.

Not surprisingly, where God was so obviously at work, other interests were challenged and they rebelled vigorously. The local silversmiths saw a threat to their trade, that of making idols of Artemis. Their fear was disguised as a threat to their local goddess and a riot ensued, money and emotions reacting against the truth and freedom of the Gospel.

There is nothing new here! It all ended up in that theatre, which was still being built at the time. Fortunately, a sensible town clerk saw to it that reason and good sense prevailed. Paul then moved on, after encouraging the new church. An extraordinary and productive two years had been fulfilled. It had been a very 'right' time and Paul had great affection for these people.

He travelled on through Troas, Macedonia, Greece, and was heading slowly back to Jerusalem. He very much wanted to speak with the Ephesian elders before he left and stopped off at Miletus, as he did not want a protracted stay in Ephesus. It was a short and easy boat trip for them then, though impossible now, as both harbours have long-since silted up. His farewell was an emotional one, in which he shared his working principles, his awareness of future problems, his clear conscience before them and a challenge to the leaders (a good message for all of us to read). He finished with pointing out the cost to himself of what he had been able to achieve with them, and a request for their prayers.

It was here at Miletus that there comes an amazing quote of Jesus – part of one verse in the middle of Acts, 'It is more blessed to give than to receive.'[4] This is the 'Transforming Principle'! It appears out of nowhere, but it had been the key to everything that he had done among them; the whole of his ministry. Where had Jesus said this? What had been its context? We have no definite answer, but suffice it to say, it sounds very 'Sermon on the Mount'. I believe it to be not just Paul's motivation, but central to the whole of any valid Christian ministry, including that of Jesus Himself. Without it, many suspect motives can creep in, as evidenced in our own times by some money-motivated, or power-hungry Christian leaders, to the disappointment and embarrassment of the Church.

I discovered it almost accidentally in 1976, while also saying a farewell. I had been involved with a Christian youth group in West London, a Crusader class (now called Urban Saints), for almost ten amazing years. This had been mainly with high school boys, who had been the action scene of some of the most encouraging and enlightening experiences that I can recall, both for them and myself! I learned how to teach teenagers biblically and was delighted to see them learn how to listen – and to respond. Many of them are still actively involved in church life.

I was convinced that God wanted me to stay with them and continue this work, but I was still a trainee surgeon looking for a permanent consultant position. Contractually, that would mean finding one within ten miles of where I

---

4. Acts 20:35.

lived. So convinced was I that I only looked and applied for posts that would not require me moving away and thus leaving this group. I was applying, but not being short-listed! Then one day, I received a letter from my professor, the shortest I had ever received: 'Dear John, Have you looked at Stafford. Ian', to which I replied with an even shorter one, 'Dear Ian, No. John'! But it was not to be ignored and provoked a lot of praying. Ian was not only my professor, but also a respected Christian. So I went and looked at the job and immediately felt right about it – it was the job I had trained for! But I still had to apply, be short-listed and then be interviewed. I was offered the job; what now?

Was God trying to say something? I accepted the position. After I had broken the news about the interview to the group, my senior leader told me that when he heard 'Stafford', he knew I was going! The reason was a bit complex, but was helpfully affirming of my decision. He was right! Many new things have come from that move.

Three months later came the time to leave. What would my last talk be? How would I say goodbye? So I spoke on Paul's farewell to the Ephesian elders in Acts 20:22-38 (which had the appropriateness of there being several young Greeks in the group!). And that is where I discovered this remarkable and all-relevant verse. Paul was reviewing his ministry by sharing himself – his involvement, working principles, deep desires and personal, practical cost. Then, there it was! A Principle that applied to everything in Christian living and working. I had never noticed it before. The more I have looked at it over the years, the more convinced I am; it is a vital key to getting life right. Also, the more I have looked at it, the more radical it appears. It challenges all that I have been taught. It is totally counter-

everything in the philosophy of our world. It is consistent with what Paul calls elsewhere 'the mind of Christ'[5] – thinking in God terms. That is big – indeed, huge.

Countercultural

We live in a grasping world. Its ethos is to get as much as you can, by whatever means you can (if you can get away with it!) and hold on to it as long as you can. Our education system is often a training ground for selfishness (though it is not polite actually to say that), being prepared for the rat race, learning to climb the ladder of success and not to be embarrassed about treading on the fingers of other people trying to do the same, or even pushing them off!

The magnitude of our acquisition is the measure of the degree of our success. Holding onto my position and trying to advance it is the continual aim. It is also the essence of sin! The Principle strongly disagrees with this philosophy: 'It cannot be sensible, right or desirable. It must therefore be wrong.' But is it?

Counter-educational

We are taught the skills for life from childhood. Look back over your own life. They are very real: maximise everything you can; be devious if necessary, but don't admit it and certainly don't get caught; everybody else is doing it too and won't stop to help, particularly if it risks their own progress. It is so nearly universal as to seem right. 'Everybody does it' is so often said, but no. Some of us do not! 'The ends justify the means' is often quoted, but almost invariably is proved wrong over history. Are 'the ends' actually worth having when we get there?

5. 1 Corinthians 2:16.

Even the morality of 'professional ethics' is often suspect. It has been described 'as the rules and principles of protecting members of that Profession from one another'! The rule remains, 'Look after Number One'. Our world is predominantly godless and this is how it lives. The eventual outcomes will turn out to be negative, indeed disastrous.

Counter-personal

'If I live by the Principle, what might happen to me?' I will be walked on. What about my rights? Indeed, who will look after my interests and defend me from others who don't live this way? And what about my preferences – what I like doing? Am I not free to live as I want? Situational Ethics arrived in the 1960s: 'If it feels good, do it.' 'I am not hurting anybody else' is very often untrue, but it is the way we say we live. Or pretend to. They were the seeds of today's postmodern philosophy. And what about my possessions? 'What's mine is mine and I can do what I like with it' might be true in law, but not in God's law. Then comes 'my job, my position, my reputation' – all my precious interests to defend and promote. Jesus spoke into this sort of thinking and gives God's answer. 'Seek His Kingdom and righteousness first; He will look after the consequences'.[6]

A very worrying area is the possessive 'my faith, my church, my role, my ministry'. Even, 'my God'! Yes, even – or particularly – in the spiritual realm, motivation can be frighteningly wrong and the Transforming Principle powerfully relevant – as Paul pointed out. Spiritual selfishness was the sin of the Pharisees, it still is. Living by rules; ticking boxes! A semblance of godliness, but without the dynamic of commitment and relationship.

6. See Matthew 6:33.

It looks so right, but is completely wrong, no matter who may be impressed. Sadly, there are many Pharisees in our churches of today – at all levels and all denominations: 'the appearance of godliness, but denying the power'.[7]

So, in every part of life, it looks as though 'What can I get out of it?' is a dangerous motive. In Christian living it is very destructive.

What made Paul tick?

Here is a man with real fire in his belly – clear-thinking, dynamic, energetic, outspoken, willing to put himself out physically and emotionally, but why? Let's take a closer look at his values, principles and motivation. We have seen him in action in Ephesus, what more can we find? A lot! He lays out his past, present and future in his letter to the Philippians – his formidable pedigree.[8] He ticked all the right boxes, culturally, educationally, religiously, enthusiastically and legally. His conclusion was (I am) 'faultless'! And he believed it! Then he became a Christian and reassessed himself.[9] Compared with what he now had, all the rest was lost profit, a handicap, or in his own (rather shocking) word, 'crap'! Yes, that is his actual word, but we are afraid to translate it. It is too strong!

He now had a completely new set of thinking and working principles. He still had his valuable education and biblical knowledge, but now had a true righteousness, 'from God' and based on faith in Christ. He had found what faith in God was all about and desired passionately for that relationship to deepen and extend into new dimensions of energy and motivation in the present. But more, to

---

7. 2 Timothy 3:5, ESV.
8. Philippians 3:4-6.
9. Philippians 3:7-11.

go beyond that into sharing in Jesus' suffering, death and even resurrection itself. Full identity in everything – righteousness, power, purpose, ministry and destiny. A taking hold through sequential self-deployment and self-sacrifice of all the purposes of God. A dynamic process of pressing on, taking hold, straining forward – to win! Total and positive commitment in giving himself. Appearing to lose everything that mattered, but finding the new dimensions of being part of God's infinity, expressed in a life of giving.

In my own small way, this had been something of the challenge to me in leaving that highly successful youth group. Apparent loss, but with what results? For me, many and often in unexpected ways. New opportunities, a new group (and church), new successes and expansion of my gifting. But what about *that group*? Had I been pseudo-altruistic, or pursuing (successfully) my career? Had I been right to leave? Who would look after them? Yes, there were problems and the group now no longer exists as such. But God is still at work in many of them that I know of. Indeed, I still work with some of them in another context. In the economy of God, nothing is wasted. He is no man's debtor.

But isn't giving risky?

Yes, very, humanly speaking! But we are not speaking humanly; we are in the God dimension. It is about giving 'without expecting to get anything back':[10]

> Lord, teach me to be generous . . .
> to give and not to count the cost . . .
> to labour and not to ask for any reward,
> save that of knowing that I do your holy will.[11]

---

10. Luke 6:35.
11. St Ignatius Loyola, www.ignatianspirituality.com/teach-me-to-be-generous/ (accessed 2 February 2023).

. . . though if we have done the right thing, there are good outcomes, certainly in the long-term and often, also more immediately.

We need to look at this from two points of view:

Principles. What guides our thinking? They may sound worthy, impressive, even commendable. They may be obviously right, but are they a bit grandiose and unrealistic? Actually, what God gives is beauty in simplicity. So watch what you are saying. Are my principles actually God's principles? Think how they might work out . . . A clear theology was important in Paul's teaching and writing. We live in times now, where a lot of Christian teaching seems shallow or facile. What actually *is* our 'gospel'?

Practice. Keeping your feet on the ground, even though your heart is in heaven. Is this giving realistic? What might it mean – in terms of deficit, or uncertainty? How far do I go? Am I generating unnecessary problems? Are there sensible limits? 'Can I afford this?' But also, can I *not* afford it? Where might it lead? Jesus tells us to be realistic in our plans and decisions.[12] He does not call us to be naïve, unthinking, irresponsible, or just plain stupid. God's way may sometimes *look* unwise, or even dangerous, but it works! Think of the Cross!

So, what is Jesus actually *calling* me to do and to be? This may start in broad principle, but is later worked out in detail for living. What is His way forward to a life that is both productive and also satisfying? The Jesus-life is always about both. We may look like losers in the short term, but always finish as winners. This is a strong theme in the book of Revelation. Jesus says, 'Well done, good and faithful

12. Luke 14:28-33.

servant . . . Enter into the joy of your lord'.[13] There are two important phrases that apply here:

- Generosity of spirit. New and released thinking. Freedom from selfishness and the misery of self-apprehension (consciously living in the limitations of self-inadequacy) and freedom to move into living in God-dimensions. He gives new perspectives into seeing what is possible, as we experience His Spirit working in our spirit. This is bigger than we can ask, think, or even imagine.[14] Then, we start to discover the joy and excitement of fulfilment.

- Generosity of action. Looking at our resources through His eyes and seeing how comprehensive they can become. 'Everything is possible for one who believes.'[15] Believing is not about living on a wish-list, it is about discovering what God actually wants – and doing it. Then we can look with a new reality at the opportunities and needs that are before us. So we can start to identify them comprehensively and realistically; to see the practicalities and what resources are needed, including personal and spiritual gifting. We can then discern whether this is our job or one for somebody else. We not called to bravado! We are called to work together. Being 'more blessed' is not a matter of being proved right or wrong, it is about motivation, attitude and consistency in thinking and behaviour; being part of the economy of God. Living out the reality of radical Christianity, as described in the Bible and

---

13. Matthew 25:21, NKJV.
14. See Ephesians 3:20.
15. Mark 9:23.

demonstrated by Jesus and His followers. It is about fulfilling my purpose and destiny, what we used to call 'saved to serve' – in all situations, with relevance, imagination and love: 'those who live should no longer live for themselves but for him who died for them and was raised again'.[16] There were many Old Testament characters who also lived this way. Daniel immediately springs to mind.

So, to the Principle, to make it into our driving motive. 'It is more blessed to give than to receive' is about going for the best because it is the way of God, not because it is my wage for serving Him!

Since discovering this simple but challenging truth, I have tried to live by it. Success has bred success; failure has not been a surprise! I am still human. Disciples are always learners and there is always more to learn. Apostles are sent out to teach what they have learned. I will try to explore this way of living in the coming pages. I will also learn more as I do so!

---

16. 2 Corinthians 5:15.

Chapter 2

The Long Form?

In the last chapter, we looked at a statement of Jesus that confronts many preconceived ideas of living – even 'Christian' living. 'It is more blessed to give than to receive.' Paul seems to pluck this statement out of nowhere, but somebody must have told him of it. Somebody who was there when Jesus said it. So probably one of His disciples; those whom He taught. Where might it fit, in the ministry of Jesus to His followers? There are two strong contending events for this – in Matthew's account of the Sermon on the Mount'[17] and Luke's 'Sermon on the Plain'.[18] Matthew was present at both, Luke at neither and they may both be the same event, differently reported. They are certainly very similar, but it is not helpful to get pedantic about it. They are Jesus' 'Teaching on Christianity'. They are basic and all-embracing, looking at what God is wanting His people to be, taking the teaching of the Old Testament and looking again at how it applies, works and grows in New Testament terms:

- **New thinking** of old concepts, discovering new interpretations of what they may mean. The mind of

---

17. Matthew 5-7.
18. Luke 6:17-49.

God is always bigger than our thinking. Jesus takes us out of 'rules' and into real 'life' – that we may 'have it to the full'.[19]

- **New dimensions** in the light of the new life and understanding that He was going to give. Moving into expanding our experiences and expectations; always on the verge of and expecting the miraculous – the reality of God in human lives.

- **New outcomes** of what 'fulfilling of the law' might mean. How does all this relate to where I am now and what God wants me to become?

We are about to take a rapid trip through this teaching, as recorded in Matthew 5-7, looking at a life of getting God's ways right, in the context of a real world that usually does not sympathise with this. Strangely, many people purport to quote this sermon, having (probably) never read or even heard all of it. It is politely believed to be a 'good thing', but only from a position of little knowledge! It may actually be much more radical than they realise, want, or would approve of! Be ready for big thinking . . .

Beautiful Attitudes

It starts with the Beatitudes, which is rather like the 'Abstract' for the whole Sermon. This is the 'Gospel for the Empty', starting in Chapter 5, verse 3, eight categories of people on whom God looks with favour and desire. Any of us can be in more than one, or even in all of these groups, and at different times; they all have consequences, or outcomes. I choose to use the 'old' word 'Blessed', because

---

19. John 10:10.

I know of no good modern equivalent. 'Happy', often used in translations, is inadequate. They are not about emotions or feelings, but about attitudes and outcomes; God is doing something in and to us as individuals. The 'blessing' is about satisfying and progressive movement into the perfection which is God's desire for all of us, and can be experienced and enjoyed even as it is happening. The initial emotion here might actually be fear! 'Am I up to this?'; 'what will happen if I am not?' We shall look briefly at each one.

The Humble-minded (v. 3). 'Blessed are the poor in spirit, for theirs is the kingdom of heaven.' We may find ourselves asking, 'Who am I to say or to do whatever my situation requires?' I am not 'big enough'. These are the very people that God is looking for. They have a holy discontent with their own limitations and failures and a deep desire for what may even seem impossible! They are not cluttered by self; so they won't spoil the kingdom. They will get on well with others who are similar-thinking. They will have space to find bigger experiences. They will complete the course.

The Bereft (v. 4). 'Blessed are those who mourn, for they will be comforted.' This is not actually a verse for funerals! It is for those who have lost their hopes. Their experiences have left them feeling weak and inadequate. Disappointment has become a way of life. They feel there is no way forward. They will be given strength. 'Comfort' is from the Latin *con fortis*, 'with strength'. It is not just a nice feeling.

The Timid (v. 5). 'Blessed are the meek, for they will inherit the earth.' Meekness is not weakness. It is more like not being pushy. Not taking what is not theirs. They are gentle and therefore able to fit in without causing upsets. These people are able to take responsibility as they are able to understand themselves and others. They get much more than they dreamed to be possible.

The Dry (v. 6). 'Blessed are those who hunger and thirst after righteousness, for they will be filled.'

Those who know what they need – being right with God. They know they are not there yet and are actively wanting to be so. They will find satisfaction, without guilt and free of wrong motives; ready to move forward; to receive and then to overflow. They will be able to help others.

The Carers (v. 7). 'Blessed are the merciful, for they will be shown mercy.' The thinking here actually comes from the Hebrew *hesed* – 'lovingkindness', frequently found in the Old Testament and usually about God. A quality that He expresses and also gives for us to do; a grace of gentle positivity. A blessing received, as it is given out – it gets bigger as we give it away.

The Morally Complete (v. 8). 'Blessed are the pure in heart, for they will see God.' Those who live transparent, uncluttered lives. They have no hidden skeletons lurking in the cupboard and are not afraid of criticism. 'God is of purer eyes that to behold evil.'[20] Seeing Him is potentially frightening, but utterly desirable. We can be ready to see glimpses in the present and much more clearly in heaven.

The Bridge-builders (v. 9). 'Blessed are the peacemakers, for they will be called children of God.'

Those who bring people, societies, nations and individuals together, sometimes at great personal cost or danger. These people are in the 'Family Business'. We bear the family

---

20. Habakkuk 1:13, NKJV.

likeness and do what our Father does. 'He himself is our peace'[21] and calls us to share it, 'bringing many sons and daughters to glory'. [22]

The Misunderstood (v. 10). 'Blessed are those who are persecuted because of righteousness, for theirs is the kingdom of heaven.' Those who are given a hard time *because* they are doing the right thing. They may be criticised as 'unrealistic', 'wrong', or 'other-worldly' (that may be right!). Such living raises questions and challenges small living in those who observe us. They may actually be jealous, or find us too hot to handle, so they ridicule and abuse by taking advantage – or even physically. Why? Ultimately because they know are wrong and are afraid to be righteous themselves. They have a hidden guilt complex. Those who have paid the price of kingdom living belong there. Jesus goes on to say 'Rejoice and be glad' in verse 12.

We should find this list hugely challenging to any small thinking, as we question our performance in each of these parameters and then recognise that we are not asked to pick and choose them. They are a package and are all in that sense 'compulsory'. This is what God is looking for. This is what it means to be a true disciple of Jesus.

The Way of the Kingdom
Jesus then goes on to look at specific details as to how these may work out in the practicalities of God's law and how we keep it. Jesus' teaching is not really 'new', but His vision is. We shall look briefly at most of what He goes on

21. Ephesians 2:14.
22. Hebrews 2:10.

to say. This is 'Jesus, on Christianity', what kingdom living looks like in a real world. We shall meet many old friends in these sayings and be prompted into re-examining the dimensions of our own beliefs and spiritual living. Is it just 'religion', or is it a defining way of life? God willing (and I think He is), we can come out at the other end as bigger, happier and more fulfilled people. Ask yourself the question: 'Am I willing to think and to change, as I learn?' Your answer will affect your progress.

I shall take an overview of the sermon by paragraphs, looking at them briefly to see the thrust of what they say, rather than doing an extensive analysis. You may find it helpful to read this in conjunction with your Bible. I have given a 'score' to each paragraph, a 'star rating' (out of three), for how clearly I see them demonstrating the Transforming Principle. This is not an indication of value or significance. You may disagree with me! Read each passage in your Bible, then see what you think.

Salt and Light. (Matthew 5:13-16)** Both have distinctive and attractive qualities, which if absent in their context are very noticeable. Positive living is vital if we are to give a clear witness to the glory of God. Ask yourself, 'Does my life bring vision and flavour to my world?'

What of the Law? (vv. 17-20)* Jesus' teaching is consistent with God's law, which is not for negotiation or compromise. It is to be obeyed totally. It is always relevant, until it is fulfilled (whatever that may mean in our current situation). Jesus' life and teaching fulfilled much of the Old Testament, particularly concerning sacrifices, but was then replaced by 'New Commandments' – God's provision for new times. Not to keep the law is serious, but doing it means much more than living by rules, the problem of the Pharisees. Rules are easier to see and tick off. Details matter, but the challenge is to bring them into real life; going beyond the routines of religion into generous living that will bring benefit to other people and also to honour God.

Problem Relationships. (vv. 21-26)* Right relationships are basic to living. Murder is an extreme example of *not* being right! However, character assassination *is* possible, starting with ill-feeling and harsh words. It is dangerous to the speaker and needs urgent resolution, or it can also become a cause of making even worship impossible. We become so cluttered with wrong living and attitudes that we cannot meet with God ourselves. The importance of forgiveness and release come up later, when Peter asked, 'how many times shall I forgive my brother or sister who sins against me? Up to seven times?' Jesus' answer, 'not seven times, but seventy-seven times',[23] was not a mathematical exercise: 'Just keep doing it!' Not releasing could also have legal consequences, which could have been avoidable.

Marital Morality. (vv. 27-32)* Faithful relationships, particularly in marriage, are the basis of a stable society. Adultery is specifically forbidden by God[24] – it is very destructive. Jesus expands its meaning into even lustful thoughts. What we see and how we behave can easily escalate from 'theoretical' sin into the real thing! Real risk requires radical action – like getting rid of an eye or a hand. Not necessarily literally, but by living as if we had.

'Legal' Oaths. (vv. 33-37)* Transparent honesty should be a hallmark of Christian living. It does not require desperate efforts at self-validation through swearing by a higher

---

23. Matthew 18:21.
24. Exodus 20:14.

authority – even God's throne! Do people respect you as a WYSIWYG – 'What You See Is What You Get'? Is your word your bond, or do people take what you say with a pinch of salt? All that is needed is a clear 'yes' or 'no'. The Christian 'giver' does not have to be afraid of standing by the consequences of their openness. It is part of investing in being right before God. In the long-term, the truth brings no fear; it will never need to apologise – to anybody.

Retribution. (vv. 38-42)** Vindictive behaviour is wrong, even if it is legal. We all want our 'rights' (whatever that means!). History is full of examples of pursuing this line, even to disastrous conclusions. It is the basis of feuds, which produce destruction of families or communities (sometimes over many generations) to unexpected and even ridiculous degrees. Jesus confronts this with the 'extra mile' principle; not just being fair, but being generous. It is beyond criticism and breaks through problem situations.

Problem People. (vv. 43-48) *** Jesus continues by looking beyond justice into love, but of whom? Even your enemies! The ones who cause you grief. Why? Because, as God's children, we may prove the reality of that relationship by doing what He does. He is the generous Giver of all things, to all people. 'God is love.'[25] We are His agents in this world, to live by His principles and to reflect His glory. We are called to go beyond duty, into breaking barriers and building bridges. 'Be perfect . . . as your heavenly Father is perfect.' That is not an option, it is a command! It is part of the 'more blessed' way. It is God's way. It must become our way, even if it is difficult.

Public Religion. (6:1-4)* Quiet generosity is magnificent. It has no axe to grind; it delights in doing the right thing,

25. 1 John 4:8-10.

because it is right. It is not about our image, or even our example. Jesus gives a sad example of getting giving wrong – by becoming a public spectacle. If that was the aim, it was achieved! But it was not what God wants. Giving (which is right and good) had been spoiled. The recipients do not even have to know. God does and He is delighted.

Praying. (vv. 5-8)* – talking with God is another activity which can have problems. Jesus again points at those who make it 'something to be seen' – a performance. Private praying should be private! What about praying together? What words do we need and how complex should they be? Do we sometimes fall into the trap of autopilot rambling words, or pseudo-spiritual empty phrases? He then gives a working model – for our private praying, but mainly for praying together: 'Our Father . . .'

The Lord's Prayer. (vv. 9-15)** A Working Model. Talking together with our heavenly Father, about anything and everything; relationship, kingdom living here and now, the basics of life – food, failure, the way ahead, being released and releasing. Forgiveness is two-way, which is a bit frightening – how good am I at forgiving? It finishes with a new, large vision of where ordinary humans fit into God's big picture (v. 13).

Fasting. (vv. 16-18)* Spiritual disciplines are about transparent living. Quietly doing the appropriate right thing in spiritual matters, with unspectacular obedience. Are we trying to impress anybody, even God? We have got it wrong! Think again.

The Big Agenda. (vv. 19-23)** What are we actually trying to do through our spiritual disciplines? What do they say about *us*? Do they actually bring 'light' into our experience?

Clear Commitment. 'No one can serve two masters' (v. 24).** This is ridiculously obvious, but too often we are obviously ridiculous in our Christianity. It is all about commitment. Is loyalty divided, in which case there will be confusion in this life and, at best, embarrassment in that to come? Is my commitment to God complete or diluted? Is He my absolute or my convenience? For all of us that is an ongoing battle, in which we become more interested in the 'receive' that the 'more blessed to give'. Resolve this tension and everything else falls into place.

Worry. (vv. 25-34)*** Jesus goes on to show us the delightful consequences of total commitment to God. Three times He tells us 'do not worry'. Why? True givers are totally cared for by the great Giver. He knows our needs already and He provides for them – and much more. Worry is the way of the world; it produces nothing and eventually destroys everything. If we 'seek first his kingdom and his righteousness', He puts all the infrastructure in place to make it possible. If that commitment is our central aim, everything else follows. God looks after the consequences of our obedience.

Criticism. (7:1-6)*** The 'speck in the eye' is so much easier to see in the other person! Understanding yourself is a better place to start examining a problem. Sort out yourself and then you may be able to help the other person. The problem may then look very different, as may the solution. Doing the wrong thing at the wrong time to the wrong person is a recipe for disaster! The other person may well have a problem, but am I fit to handle it? Do I need to change first? How?

Asking and Receiving. (vv. 7-12)*** 'Do to others, what you would have them do to you'. This verse is in an odd position! It seems to sum up all that has gone before. Verses 7-11 are very much like the Transforming Principle! It is about getting life right, starting with finding God's mind – ask, seek, knock' – then blessing the other person. Use your own preferences to lead you into blessing others. 'This sums up the Law and the Prophets' – it is all that God asks.

Being Real. (vv. 15-23)* What does your life produce? Fruit defines the nature of a tree, the health of the tree and the destiny of the tree. So with us. Are we false in any way – wolves 'in sheep's clothing'? We can be – even spectacularly so! 'Did we not prophesy in your name'? The truth is visible to anyone who looks. What do other people see in me?

Hearing and Doing. (vv. 24-27)** The house on the rock story is about the outcome of the Transforming Principle: 'What have I done with the teaching of Jesus?' It is the only question that matters, because it has clear consequences; security, without fear or embarrassment. Or total disaster! The choice is ours.

These and Jesus' other teachings are the resources from which Christian living works. He brings a breath of fresh air to old ways, which as God's law, had started well, but had become corrupted. True righteousness is about fulfilling all that God asks; the law not as a confining prison, but as a framework for freedom.

- 'False righteousness' is a misnomer – indeed an oxymoron! It was typified by the Pharisees who thought they were doing all the right things, but had reduced them to rules. Ticking boxes is a much easier way to live, because you know what you have done and when you have got there. The rules may not be the reality of what the law says, just an interpretation. You can even find yourself ticking non-existent boxes! It is easier to see things than to live spirituality, but spirituality is the ultimate reality. It stands together with God and he endorses it.

- 'Self-righteousness' is an extension of this. 'Because I have ticked all the boxes, I am alright, indeed I am an upright and fine example of what God wants.' It sticks in the throat to hear it, but some people honestly believe it. They may also convince others. These two (indeed related) attitudes are not left in the past. They are still very much with us, even in Churches, even in actual Christians! As William Temple is reported to have said, 'it is possible to be righteous repulsively'! They eventually stand naked and exposed; they are working from a bankrupt account. They will find themselves embarrassed before God, with nowhere to hide; also ashamed before men, because they have missed out on the very things they were claiming.

Jesus came to release those whose religion had become wrapped in rules, rituals and routines; to transform traditions, to turn routines into relationship, doing into being and becoming. Boring has become beautiful, as a new spirituality becomes expressed in a new mentality and new reality.

Maybe the right place to finish this chapter is to return to the question asked earlier: 'Am I willing to think and to change, as I learn?'

Chapter 3

The Jesus Way

In the previous chapter we looked at Jesus' basic teaching for those who follow Him; his 'Outline Principles for Christianity'. We now have to go back a little in His programme for action. After thirty-something years as 'the carpenter's son' and then as 'the Carpenter',[26] it was time for Him to go public; to enter the purpose for which He had been prophesied and born, in specific terms.

John (the Baptist) was at work by the Jordan River receiving people who wanted to start a new life and to mark it by a public event; repentance, a change in thinking and living from old ways and then, baptism (this was a well-recognised format, the Jewish *Mikvah,* a ceremonial washing). Then ... over the hill walked Jesus. John stopped, looked and called out, 'See, the Lamb of God that takes away the sin of the world.[27] and went on to baptise Him; an identification with those He had come to save into fullness of life. Was this also time for a big speech and a spectacular beginning? No, it was a time to be 'led' into the desert by the Holy Spirit, to be tested,[28] as the man who was God. Forty days of fasting, then challenges to His commitment,

---

26. Matthew 13:55; Mark 6:3.
27. John 1:29. Author translation.
28. Matthew 4:1-11.

identity and motivation – a focusing of His mind before starting His ministry. Satan raised 'if' questions, casting doubt as to whether He was really the Son of God. He tempted Him to easy answers that might ultimately avoid the necessity of the cross. He even offered Him 'all the kingdoms of the world' if He would worship him! They were not actually his to give – they already belonged to the God who created them, who now stood before him! Worship is not appropriate to a created being anyway. Satan, 'the father of lies',[29] seems not to have realised the stupidity of all this, when confronting the Truth in person!

Then came the time for the big speech – His first sermon in His home synagogue. The 'Nazareth Manifesto' in which He identifies himself with Isaiah's prophecy of the Messiah: 'The Spirit of the Lord God is on me, because he has anointed me to proclaim good news . . . freedom . . . recovery of sight . . . to set the oppressed free . . . the year of the Lord's favour.'[30] He finished up with 'Today this . . . is fulfilled': 'This is me!' His claim was clear. The reaction was rapid; rejection and attempted execution, for blasphemy. He moved on quickly and continued the ministry that we see in the Gospels; that of preaching, teaching and healing, including driving out demons. He then called His team 'disciples' to learn from Him and to work with Him. They were the ones who received the teaching of the Sermon on the Mount, to define and direct their calling by Jesus.

We see all the time that what He taught, He did. So, how did that demonstrate the 'Transforming Principle'? It was in what Paul described as His 'attitude', His way of thinking which led into action:

29. John 8:44.
30. Luke 4:14-30.

Christ Jesus: who, being in very nature God,
did not consider equality with God something to be
used to his own advantage;
rather, he made himself nothing
by taking the very nature of a servant,
being made in human likeness.
And being found in appearance as a man,
he humbled himself
by becoming obedient to death –
even death on a cross![31]

Attitude determines action and is defined by it. So what does Paul show us here? How is it that Jesus' life was His visual aid? There are three main features. He was:

Selfless. He was God and He knew it. His identity as God was by nature equality. It was not a position of strength and security acquired by violence or usurpation. It was what He was. Indeed, it was by choice that He would release many of His rights and privileges, as God in the short term, to achieve His ministry, expressing His 'mind' in very clear criteria. He started by being born as a man, with all the limitations that that would have. That was essential in being able to achieve our salvation.

Serving. By progressive releasing, He stepped out of the privileges of infinity into real, practical humanity. So, we see Him born in a smelly stable as a dependent baby; God in a dirty diaper! Growing up in a peasant family in an unimportant town that was often used as a joke.[32] Later, as an incipient teenager He had to learn family responsibility

---

31. Philippians 2:5-8.
32. John 1:46.

and obedience.[33] His humanity meant that He was limited in time and place, also in knowledge of some 'God things'. As an adult, He gave Himself to the needs of others (a huge variety of them) in practical care and loving understanding. He was a manual worker, supporting His mother and siblings. He mixed with people, including all the wrong people – the poor, the dispossessed, the rejected of society, with the sick and also the blatantly 'sinful', with social outcasts, even with the 'unclean' – He actually touched lepers! He also knew some upper-class people and Roman officers. He gave time to children and foreigners. But there was more . . . The final steps.

Sacrificial. His call was not to be a philosopher, a philanthropist, or even a theologian, it was to be the 'Saviour of the world'[34] and that would have a very clear direction and conclusion. It would progress through humanity to humility, to obedience, to death; and that of the most horrendous kind, 'even death on a cross', a Roman execution. Physically and emotionally devastating, humiliating and degrading as He hung naked and ridiculed in full public gaze. I know of no painting or sculpture that has ever attempted to show that full truth and no church that would ever allow it to be displayed!

But what was happening here? This was not just a man; this was God! A spiritual event, with Trinitarian consequences, as Jesus cried to His Father, 'My God, my God, why have you forsaken me?'[35] What was He doing? Peter tells us that 'He himself bore our sins' in his body on the cross'.[36] The Saviour of the world, bearing the

---

33. Luke 2:41-52.
34. 1 John 4:14.
35. Matthew 27:46.
36. 1 Peter 2:24.

consequences of our sin. 'Christ also suffered once for sins, the righteous for the unrighteous, to bring you to God.'[37] The Ultimate Giver had no limits to His giving.

> Come, see His hands and His feet,
> The scars that speak of sacrifice.
> Hands that flung stars into space,
> To cruel nails surrendered.
> This is our God . . .[38]

But is that the end of the story? Certainly not! We go back to Philippians 2. There was a:

Sequel. 'Therefore God exalted him to the highest place and gave him the name that is above every name, that at the name of Jesus every knee should bow . . . and every tongue acknowledge that Jesus Christ is Lord, to the glory of God the Father.'[39] A cosmic outcome, for what Jesus did was not just for time and humanity, but for the whole suffering universe.[40] Having completed His task, He returned to His eternal pre-eminence, the highest place in heaven. And the response? Universal recognition and worship, to the glory of God – whether willingly, or forced by circumstances in eternity.

There is now a man in Heaven, doing what? Preparing a place for us,[41] praying for us[42] and extending His grace.[43] Where would we have been if He had not done all this?

---

37. 1 Peter 3:18.
38. 'The Servant King', Graham Kendrick, Copyright © 1983 Thankyou Music.
39. Philippians 2:9-11.
40. Romans 8:22.
41. John 14:2.
42. Hebrews 7:25.
43. Hebrews 4:16.

'Without hope and without God in the world.'[44] But He did! So where are we now, what difference should it make?

Paul's 'hymn' is preceded by a very significant passage.[45] It starts with four 'ifs' and this is very clear in the Greek, though not in some translations. 'If any encouragement in Christ, any comfort from love' ... 'any fellowship of the Holy Spirit'[46] ... 'any affection and sympathy'. Implied questions, to which the answer may be 'no'. We need to ask them of ourselves, because they will determine where we stand and what we should then be doing ...

'Am I united with Christ – am I a Christian?' That means taking a step of commitment; a response of obedience. The 'how' and the 'when' of that is unique to each one of us. For many of us this is process, rather than a clear point in time. A call, a choice and a decision. Entering into a new relationship with God. What a privilege!

'Do I experience the strengthening and stability of His love?' To become, to be and to do what God wants. The beginning of a new lifestyle.

'Am I in fellowship with the Holy Spirit?' Knowing His motivation and power as a working reality. Enabled, empowered and directed into the will and ways of God. A new life with new possibilities.

'Am I warm-hearted towards others?' Outgoing, unrestricted; a 'Giver', in happy and helpful interrelationship.

What, then, should all that look like? It should show in the way we function individually and together as Christians:

Unity. In mind, in love, in spiritual identity and in purpose together as Christians.

---

44. Ephesians 2:12.
45. Philippians 2:1-2.
46. NKJV.

Motivation. Unselfish in releasing our desires, resources, privileges and position. Generous in sharing ourselves through our new nature in Jesus.

Relationships. Respect, humility and realistic care as we live and work together.

All this adds up to: 'Your attitude should be the same as Jesus.'[47] What might that look like? Being Just like Jesus and just like the 'Transforming Principle', 'It is more blessed to give than to receive'. What might it then do? It will do what Jesus did! It will live a life that is:

Selfless. From a position of genuinely knowing who and what we are, a position of privilege, as those who have benefited from what Jesus has done. Children of God Himself, living life by the power of the Holy Spirit, citizens of heaven, God's agents – willing and wanting to be givers; to deploy ourselves in an outward-looking life, blessing other people. This means making a deliberate choice.

> Take my life and let it be
> Consecrated Lord, to Thee . . .'[48]

Called by God to live the Jesus-life in a hostile world that desperately needs salvation. To pay what it takes to fulfil the will of God, because it is my desire to do and to be what is right. Living 'like Jesus':

Serving. No 'airs', or self-importance, no matter whoever we are, whatever we are called to do, or whenever that may be. We may be misunderstood or misrepresented. There is nothing new here. It was Jesus' experience and

---

47. See Philippians 2:5.
48. Frances Ridley Havergal (1836-79). 'Take My Life and Let it Be'.

has also been that of His people throughout the ages, to the present. 'The message of the cross is foolishness to those who are perishing'.[49] But remember too that 'The foolishness of God is wiser than human wisdom'.[50] It always turns out to be right in the long-term.

We are part of a great heritage – servants of the God of history; identified with the Old Testament saints, and even more clearly, with those of the New Testament. Part of the long line of God's people through the ages, and accepting that identity, including that of those who suffered and even died for their faith – and still do.

Sacrificial. That too! Giving as much as it takes, with no limits, bearing the image of Christ.[51] 'Being Jesus' wherever we are, in time, place, situation, or company. Always 'on duty' – no 'time off', or holiday breaks, reflecting His reality. Being part of the purposes of God. Living like this is redemptive, it communicates the power of Jesus today, it delivers the saving message, it leads people to Him. But sacrifice costs; it is the ultimate in giving; it is the ultimate in achieving. And yes, there is a cost.

Sequel. Jesus said, 'Because I live, you also will live.'[52] He also said, "I am the resurrection and the life. The one who believes in me will live, even though they die; and whoever lives by believing in me will never die.'[53] This is big stuff! Glory does not come cheaply, but it is of infinite value. The path to it is that of 'cheerful givers'.[54] Jesus' way for Himself was the Transforming Principle and He calls us to follow Him in it. It is the defining hallmark of God's people.

---

49. 1 Corinthians 1:18.
50. 1 Corinthians 1:25.
51. 2 Corinthians 3:18.
52. John 14:19.
53. John 11:25-26.
54. 2 Corinthians 9:7.

Chapter 4

The Nature of God

God is the ultimate giver . . . The Trinity gives within itself in eternal relationship, existing even before the creation of the universe, but also looks outwards to extend that relationship with other rational beings, to make an even bigger creation. That seems to have begun with the angels, but the nature of that relationship is not clearly defined ('He makes his angels spirits, and his servants flames of fire.'[55]) God's thinking was much bigger than that. The created universe followed. Givers love to give beyond themselves and the creation was generated by God as an opportunity to give wide and large. This goes far beyond any misconception that the universe is a toy for God to play with, or that humans give him the opportunity to manipulate them. The evidence is that He really loves what He has made and enjoys sharing it with its population. That started with one, then two people, with the plan that they should multiply, to inhabit the earth and also participate in running it.[56] His conclusion was that it was all 'very good'.[57] God actually delights in what He has made, and that includes you and me. He even gave us a special day (Sabbath) to celebrate that.

---

55. Hebrews 1:7.
56. Genesis 1:27-28.
57. Genesis 1:31.

St Paul tells us that in us God wanted relationship, not servitude, 'that [people] would seek him and perhaps reach for him and find him',[58] not because He had any needs. He is in relationship already and loves it. His desire for that is a continuing and expanding one.

Paul was speaking in Athens, where there was very little concept of who God was and what He wants. He actually quotes another of their poets, who saw Him mainly as the great Provider 'In him we live and move and have our being'.[59] Although a pagan, he was right and his statement is worth our notice; another reminder that God is the Giver, without whom we could not even exist.

Paul had started this discussion with the Greek philosophers with 'he himself gives everyone life and breath and everything else'.[60] The scope of God's giving is complete and universal – all things needed and for all people. There isn't anything else, but we know that the 'everything' includes salvation and 'life ... to the full'.[61] He is the continuing Giver, not just of the obvious necessities, but of all that makes life special, enjoyable and fulfilling. Life is supposed to achieve. It has been created in almost profligate variety; God seems to love variety. The Athenians had been regarding Paul's teaching as a bit of a joke when he started. He wisely back-pedalled and recommenced from more familiar ground (a lesson we could often take to heart). He could them pick up on the Genesis story, without mentioning Genesis! 'The God who made the world ... the Lord of heaven and earth',[62] the God who 'from one man ... made all the nations ... that they would seek him ... and

---

58. Acts 17:27.
59. Acts 17:28.
60. Acts 17:25.
61. John 10:10.
62. Acts 17:24.

42

find him . . . he is not far from any one of us'.[63] This God is interested in giving to everybody, in delighting all humans.

Why is God so interested, even in people who do not believe, or even positively deny Him? St John explains to Christians the basic truth that 'God is love',[64] which Paul gets to by another route – it is extended to those who do not deserve it! So, what is 'love'? English, and many other languages, have only one word for it, which has to cover a range of meanings from pleasant feelings, personal preferences, emotional attachment, family relationships, to wild passion! The Greek language has four words, well-described by C.S. Lewis in *The Four Loves*.[65]

The word widely used in the New Testament, is *agape* (three syllables). This is the love that God expresses, the one about which we are talking. It is the love that loves to give, that is the way it is expressed. It is totally unselfish. It has no hidden agenda, or suspect undercurrents. It can even survive without being reciprocated. It can take rejection without being angry or vengeful. It is willing to give time for rethinking and possible change. It has no limits.[66] It is the love that is God's nature, the love that He has for His creation and the love that He has for the Church.[67] It is not just a nice feeling; it has strong emotion within it. He really cares. Love is objective; God, the great Giver, does things to and for those whom He loves. He does this with great care, relevance and imagination.

So, what else does Paul tell us? Love generates love and demonstrates its effectiveness in new life and new living. Not to love each other is not to be in relationship with

63. Acts 17:26-27.
64. 1 John 4:8.
65. C.S. Lewis, *The Four Loves* (London: HarperCollins, 2002).
66. 1 Corinthians 13:4-8.
67. Ephesians 5:25-27.

God either![68] The proof of love and its extent is that Jesus was deputed to bring new Life at God's expense. Love is grace in action, a propitiation by paying the price of sin and the consequences of God's judgement, from within Himself; undeserved and not earned. St Paul writes of love in comprehensive terms as 'the most excellent way'.[69] Faith and hope are also great Christian virtues, 'but the greatest ... is love.'[70] It is eternally relevant.

In the Old Testament, the widely used word for this love is *hesed*, often translated as 'lovingkindness'. Both this and *agape* speak, at their best, of a two-way relationship. Love loves to give and to be reciprocated. This receiving back is not wrong. It is not trying to buy God's favour. It does not deny the 'Transforming Principle'; indeed, it reinforces it. One-way relationships are ultimately doomed; marriage being an important example. Both partners commit to love, through all circumstances. Paul points out that it is a reflection of the relationship between Christ and His Church,[71] unlike many marriages, which sadly run out of love.

Love is not a vague word, it has all-embracing criteria. It is patient, kind, unselfish, humble. Polite, generous, protecting, expectant and persevering. 'Love never fails',[72] it 'is as strong as death'[73] and actually continues beyond it, into God's eternity. These are very practical realities. But it is also frightening to realise that it is possible to step outside love. The justly famous Romans 8 gives is a glorious affirmation of God's love, 'I am convinced that ... [nothing] will be able to separate us from the love of God that is

---

68. 1 Corinthians 12:3.
69. 1 Corinthians 12:31.
70. 1 Corinthians 13:13.
71. Ephesians 5:32.
72. 1 Corinthians 13:8.
73. Song of Solomon 8:6.

in Christ Jesus our Lord.'[74] This is true, but God's loving safekeeping is not a prison. It is a dynamic participation and we can opt out! Whatever the reason, we can step outside the protection of the love of God (though He still loves us). This is frightening! There will be disastrous consequences, but the fault is not with God. That is the story of the world and sadly, even of the history of God's people. It still happens. Praise God that His love continues; He does not give up on us. We can come back.

Sin entered the world when the magnificence of the primaeval love between God and humanity was violated by a deliberate, knowing choice. To try to attain a new state of imagined being 'like God'.[75] Desire grew into disobedience; stepping beyond the boundaries of mutual love. The immediate result was the breaking of relationship – from humanity's end, demonstrated by embarrassment, fear and hiding. Humankind has been hiding from God ever since. It was not until the 'second Adam'[76] came that the relationship was restored through salvation. The door of communication was opened for all who would choose to enter it. Jesus declared 'greater love has no one than this: to lay down one's life for one's friends. *You are my friends if you do what I command* . . . This is my command: love each other.'[77] Get back into relationship. New sons and daughters of God, with new lives to live, in new dimensions and a New Commandment to live by – the family motto. John carries this through into his first letter, 'since God so loved us, we also ought to love one another'.[78] God is the Great Lover and His children bear the family likeness.

---

74. Romans 8:38-39.
75. Genesis 3:5.
76. See 1 Corinthians 15:22.
77. John 15:13-14,17, emphasis mine.
78. 1 John 4:11.

45

It defines His people: 'By this everyone will know that you are my disciples, if you love one another.'[79] This is our mandate – to be givers, like our Father; to love even those who do not deserve it. But what does He receive for this? By most of humanity, rejection; we try to live the lie of self-sufficiency, ignoring, refusing, or maybe offering terms or limits, to any response. Are Christians any better? Sadly, history has often showed remarkable fickleness (amid some outstanding successes).

When love is spurned, what happens? Humans may react in different ways, but usually there is anger and often a desire to 'get even', or a decision not to be hurt again. God is different. He is not vindictive. He is more sad, or disappointed, than angry, and longs for restoration. He does everything in His power to achieve this; we have seen the cost. The prophecy of Hosea is a picture of this and His efforts to regain the love of His people. A marriage broken by adultery and the offending wife bought back in a slave market by a still-loving husband. Jesus wept over Jerusalem.[80] He looked back on their history of rejecting their loving God and forward to the destruction that would happen less that forty years later. This was an expression of distraught love! A love that would buy back His people at His own expense, a few days later.

The letter to the Laodiceans tells of a not-unusual state of affairs. A former Christian enthusiasm, which had cooled off into mediocrity: 'you are lukewarm – neither hot nor cold'[81] – 'You make me sick!' says Jesus. Actually, He would like us to be boiling (the Greek for 'zealous'[82])! The great Giver wants us to be like Him – full-on, hot and strong.

---

79. John 13:35.
80. Luke 19:41.
81. Revelation 3:16.
82. Revelation 3:19, ESV.

Love has plans! Even from before there was a problem, the concept and details of salvation were in existence. The seeds of the gospel were already declared immediately after the Fall. The Tempter himself would be overcome and his plans would come to nothing, but at a cost.[83] Love is willing to pay. It will go all the way necessary to restore relationship. The loving father of the Prodigal Son, though devastated by what had happened and aware of what was likely to happen, lived in hope.[84] He was waiting and ready; love does that. He might be disappointed and not see the sad return, but he was constantly read to run, embrace, forgive and restore. What a picture of the God who loves!

The book of Revelation takes the account of salvation right through to its fulfilment and completion (if eternity actually is a 'completion'!). God always completes what He starts. Much of it is difficult to understand and there have been many interpretations of varying helpfulness. Its contents are maybe more about encouragement than detailed understanding. The style of writing in its latter half is very much like a fantasy story; it is in picture language (*mythopoeia*); though with factual content – a classic love story finishing. That seductive snake in Genesis had now become a fearsome monster and the subtleties of temptation have grown into full-on vindictiveness and desire for the destruction of all that a loving God stands for. The final message of Revelation is, we win!

That is the astounding truth about the God whose love transcends all and overcomes all. What He starts, He finishes. We can choose in, or opt out. God will respect our choice, even though deeply saddened if it is for disaster.

---

83. Genesis 3:15.
84. Luke 15:11-24.

So, 'God is love'[85] and love, by nature, gives continually. Love is the basis of the 'Transforming Principle' – it is a mentality of giving which becomes relevantly and comprehensively practical. When we become givers, we are expressing the nature of the Father God at work within us. We learn to live by God's principles, we start to enter into living in God dimensions and then to see God results. Miracles? Yes, of all shapes and sizes, starting with new life in Jesus and extending into all situations, needs and opportunities into which God will lead us.

---

85. 1 John 4:8.

Chapter 5

Who Am I?

With God, nobody is a 'nobody'! But with Him, I have a past, a present and a future. We all do.

Many people have significant problems in their past – a not-so-good family, an undesirable community in which to be raised, bad health, accidental circumstances, maybe even an unhelpful church. What rises in your own mind? Are there things which make you feel unvalued, unwanted, disappointed, angry, insecure, useless? Many people feel undervalued or underprivileged, even about things that are not their fault. That can have continuing negative effects, which limit even Christian freedom and joy and provoke ineffectiveness in serving God – 'I can't, because . . .' Because what? Do you see it? Do you acknowledge it? That is the first step to resolving it.

When Jesus steps into a life, everything can change. When and how that happens is different for all of us – we are all unique, but there are similarities. They may be expressed as 'by grace you have been saved through faith . . . not by works'; 'it is the gift of God'.[86] God has done something for us that we could not do for ourselves. Jesus died for our sins and if we put our trust in Him, we will be 'saved', not by own cleverness, because some of us aren't,

---

86. Ephesians 2:8-9.

but as a gift that God has paid for in Jesus. That is our new present – 'created in Christ Jesus to do good works, which God prepared in advance for us to do'[87] – right with God and a new life begun. All of us have to take this step. It is the key that opens up new ways and new possibilities.

Then comes a whole new future – the work to do that God has specifically in mind for us to be doing, with and for Him! We become significant participants in what He is doing in His world. That started with two people,[88] and still continues . . . You may find it helpful to use two (very) brief prayers of Paul. He started with: 'Who are you, Lord'? Answer: 'I am Jesus'.[89] He then said, 'What shall I do . . . ?' Answer 'Get up . . . and go!'[90] And he went! It would cost him his status, his security and eventually, his life. It would bless the whole world – to this day.

God can even use our past experience to inform our present service opportunities. Even the negative things (like Paul), from which we may be able to help other people with similar problems. Maybe you still have hang-ups from the past, but you can relax now and find answers. Do you have somebody that you can talk and pray with? Forgiven sin is genuinely forgiven, even if Satan tries to dig it up and beat you with it (he is not called 'the accuser'[91] for nothing!). These are biblical facts, which have become historical – borne out in the real lives of countless real people, but you have to choose into them. God wants us, but we have to be willing to step out.

You can then find a way forward. Start taking faith-opportunities as God presents them to you and step out

87. Ephesians 2:10.
88. Genesis 1:27-28.
89. Acts 22:8.
90. Acts 22:10.
91. Revelation 12:10.

into knowing His call on your life, with everything put together properly. The word for it is 'peace', but it is much bigger in the Bible than we have in English (and many other languages). Even the Greek word used for it in the New Testament (*eirene*) is too small. The Bible writers were mainly Jews and the language they were thinking in was Hebrew. Their word is *shalom,* a huge word about what God does in our lives as He puts the mess of the past back together, so He can mobilise us in new ways. This is much more than a state of mind, or nice feelings. It is about:

Restoration. Life being repaired and remade, re-equipped and redirected. Jesus says, 'I [make] everything new.'[92] What a relief! Even the past faults in our nature become overtaken by God at work in us. Past negatives can become useful positives; useful experience or what to do now – or not to do!

Completeness. A whole range of God's resources become focused in real humans. A life full of new experiences and new understanding. We become much more than we were. Bigger people with bigger possibilities, as God enables and activates us by His Holy Spirit.

Integration. Everything brought together in full working order – physical, emotional and spiritual – enabled to do what God wants of us. That is what *shalom* actually means. It will grow with time, experience and obedience. More and more, we find Him to be the God of new possibilities, though we have to learn to break through our fears and sense of inadequacy. Even the pain from our past can become productive. It is almost as though God has become

---

92. Revelation 21:5.

bigger, though that of course, is ridiculous! It is just that we see Him so much more clearly.

As God calls us into becoming bigger people than we were, so He can use us as He directs us. When and how all that happens is different for all of us. I came to faith as a fifteen-year-old over a period of about six months. Three years before, I had met real Christians. I liked what I saw and started looking for it. I wanted what they had. I was invited to join a church youth group and started following what God was showing me (though that was not the way I would have expressed it at the time). Other people come earlier and some later, either quickly or slowly. What has been your experience? This is the beginning of a process which lasts all our lives. It is called 'sanctification', being made 'holy', which may sound strange. It just means made special for God (and a bit like Jesus – increasingly).

There is now a new relationship with God through Jesus. No longer is He a distant stranger, seemingly rather detached from our reality, he is now our Father, who happens to be the King of the universe! And us? His children – members of the Royal Family. We have significance and dignity. Also responsibility. Does that all sound a bit grandiose? Maybe it is, but look further. 'You are a chosen people, a royal priesthood, a holy nation, God's special possession'. Peter adds '. . . that you may declare the praises of him who called you . . .'[93] We are kingdom-builders; agents for action, with royal authority, the commissioning by Jesus to be doing His work. 'All authority . . . has been given to me. Therefore go'[94] – these are words of Jesus to His Team, sometimes called

---

93. 1 Peter 2:9.
94. Matthew 28:18-19.

'the Great Commission'. With all this come the resources of God to do the job and a passport into His world, to do anything, anytime, anywhere. 'You will be my witnesses . . .'[95] (Is this a statement or a command? Yes!) We are called into His service, representing Him in the way we live and speak. Do you actually expect God to ask anything of you? Would you like Him to? How mobile are you prepared to be? What will you say to Him? Talk to Him about it – we call it 'praying'.

God calls us to a new normality, existence and purpose through Jesus: 'Peace be with you! As the Father has sent me, I am sending you.'[96] So that is where we can be now. We have new dimensions to discover:

Identity. We do not have to feel inferior or embarrassed any more. God has made each of us unique, not for comparing ourselves with others, but for specific activity – worldwide, if necessary! Don't be scared – be what God has made you; His children and His agents in His world.

Connections. Colleagues together in the Faith, 'workers together with Him'.[97] God usually calls us to team up with others, discovering and working with those of like mind. This may be local (normally in a church context), or anywhere. There can be big surprises! Find people who can help you and who you can help.

Abilities. Those 'natural' ones we were born with and those we have discovered through our education and experience. Through release from our past inadequacies and inabilities, they can be transformed into new dimensions in our new life. They take on new qualities, dimensions and usefulness.

---

95. Acts 1:8.
96. John 20:21.
97. 2 Corinthians 6:1, NKJV.

Spiritual Gifts. These are new abilities that come direct from God, the Holy Spirit, to do the job we are called to. They are the 'tool box' that He provides for going beyond our natural abilities, or to transform them to do whatever is needed. We each have a different set, to do what we are called to. We are normally called to do that together with other people and their tool boxes. They are there to make us effective, not superior!

Does all that make you feel better? Or maybe a bit of a freak? No, we have become the most real humans we have ever been. We actually achieving true 'normality'. We are doing what humans were originally designed for – helping to run God's world. It is the rest of the world that has the problem. They are living below His intention. God could change them too – if they want it. We are in the position to live out the Transforming Principle, learning to give ourselves, so that other people may find it too.

It is God's call to be what we are and to use what we have been given:

a) His grace, that has changed us and continues to remake and renew us. We have become bigger and more usable. It will continue to expand as we learn to say 'yes' to his promptings.

b) His grace to share with others in God's world, using God's resources, as His agents for transformation.

This is all about living our normality and ability really well, to God's glory and for the blessing of other people. To live without fear and with expectation. As we have seen already, 'God . . . works in you to will and to act in order to fulfil his good purpose.'[98] You discover that in the economy of God, nothing is wasted – not even you!

We Christians are the only people who know that we can be givers and can actually afford to. God calls us to a destiny – individual ministry, together with others, to change our 'personal world', our sphere of influence and the world at large. Is that how you see yourself? It is what you are! How are you progressing? What is the next step?

---

98. Philippians 2:13.

Chapter 6

What Am I?

We have seen that God can and wants to do remarkable things in our lives. When and how He brings that new enabling and integration is different for each of us. But what is the way forward from there? We will now look more at our *identity* and our resources. Both are expanding entities, as God re-makes us as bigger people with bigger possibilities. What has God made me already? That goes back to my beginnings and my development – before and after birth.

I am a *physical* being – you could assess me by all five senses. We have a recognisable physique, which may well not be that of an Olympic athlete. Indeed, for most of us it may well be the reverse and that can be a big problem for some! There may be obvious physical inadequacies, which may cause us embarrassment, even if the problem looks bigger to us than it does to others. That is often the case; our own self-perception can colour our whole thinking and bring on feelings of inadequacy and hopelessness. 'If only I did not have . . .' whatever *it* is. Which can subtly lead into 'I can't . . . because . . .' or, 'Does God really love me, if I am like this?' The problem may be a health one, maybe from birth, or childhood, or a result of illness or accident (producing long-term physical effects, or maybe psychological difficulties). The challenge is to break through the fear of embarrassment, which may be even to the extent of not talking to God about it – does He care, is He interested, am I just stuck with it? It can be helpful to pray and be specific with God. Say it like it is! Speaking with a trusted friend may also be releasing.

We are also *psychological* beings – we have a mind and a personality, which are quite complex:

Our *intellect* is to do with thinking, understanding and learning. God has given us all minds to use and to develop. That is why we have education and training – including in Christian understanding.

Emotions are things that some men pretend they do not have! But they are an important part of all of us and express our personality; how we feel, appreciate and communicate. Sometimes those feelings can become hard to control and may embarrass us, or others. They can also be coloured (sometimes excessively) by preferences, desires and what we think other people are thinking of us.

Our *will* is the decision-making part of our minds, expressing choice that comes from perceptions from our past experience, or present understanding. We are constantly making decisions, some of them from very mixed motives – personal preferences, our perception of the expectations of others and increasingly, what God may be saying. Again, people are different here, some rushing into things without proper consideration, or maybe the opposite: 'Why can't you make up your mind?'

Although not recognised by many people, we are also *spiritual* beings; more than just the recognisable physical individual with their personality, both of which disappear at the end of life. Spirituality is about the real 'me', my eternal identity that relates with other spirits, be they human, God, or evil spirits. This is often a neglected or ignored part of our being and that will result in inadequate perception and use of our whole being. We then behave as part-people and only for the present – effectively we have no perception of a real future. That will have its results, particularly in terms of our significance now and destiny later. It will devalue and limit our present to a life of physical and psychological existence only. Both are good, but as we get older, death becomes not just an increasing reality, but a huge threat. If there is 'nothing beyond', then what we have now is ultimately meaningless. That is the philosophy of the atheist and is severely negatively encouraging! Much of our present thinking and behaving may turn out to be expressions of irrelevance, insignificance and repressed fear. We need to see and think bigger – more in God dimensions. He has made us as amazing, complex beings and normal function sees all these aspects working as one – not as separate 'compartments'. St Paul prayed for his readers, 'May your whole spirit, soul and body be kept blameless',[99] a functioning totality. Note that sin affects the 'all' and so does salvation.

All these aspects of our humanity need to develop. Just as we do not stay as children, we need to develop in our totality, to 'grow up into Christ'.[100] If that is what I have been made as a human being, what then becomes possible in what God has remade me as a Christian? All the parameters of our humanity are touched. I have a unique

99.   1 Thessalonians 5:23.
100. Ephesians 4:15, NET.

identity. I am the only one of 'me' and the same is true for you. We all have similarities and differences; unique but valid. These are things to celebrate and use.

Physically. As part of our being, we need not be afraid or ashamed to talk to God about this. He wants to use us as we are and also as we develop. Healing and empowerment involve common sense action like rest, good diet and if necessary, medical care. It may also involve God's intervention. We are often afraid or embarrassed to be open to miracles!

Psychologically God can renew and remake us bringing stability and *shalom.* Inner strength, perception and positivity. Our people-skills will be enabled, making for better relationships and a new perception of what we could do in becoming givers of what we are. There may well be people who need that from us. No longer being fearful introverts, but able to look outwards into Christian involvement. Unafraid, because God's 'perfect love drives out fear'.[101]

Spiritually, whole new dimensions open up, as this neglected part of our being rises out of its dead state and springs into the new life that we have 'to the full'.[102] The future opens up too; life has a purpose and a direction. It is not about drifting aimlessly and out of control through time and circumstances and then falling off the far end. It is about moving forwards and upwards, fulfilling the will of God as kingdom-builders; significant agents in a world living in irrelevance and meaninglessness, 'without hope and without God'.[103]

But there is more. God's intention is not just the pleasure of vigorous individuality, it extends first into *family*, His

---

101. 1 John 4:18.
102. John 10:10.
103. Ephesians 2:12.

family, the Royal Family, 'fellow workers'[104] Members together of 'the body of Christ',[105] each with our own part to fulfil in achieving the whole of what God has in mind. This is the church, a whole new vision for identity and involvement.

Not just belonging as Family, but functioning as *Team*. In the Gospel narratives, we see Jesus calling people to join Him; making up the Twelve, then seventy (two),[106] to send them out. We come in one by one ('to all who did receive him, to those who believed in his name, he gave the right to become children of God'[107]), but immediately enter into something much bigger, more interesting and more exciting than living a lonely, solo existence. We are God's family, doing God's business, with God's resources, from the Family account. Are you experiencing this? But we are not just changed people, we also have a new outlook and, to make that function are given new resources to make that outlook happen. All these aspects of 'being' need to grow in an interactive and cohesive way, to produce balanced individuals in healthy relationship. What does this mean?

My greatest resource after God, is myself. The Transforming Principle therefore starts with me, 'It is more blessed to give . . .' and, although giving is always personal, what does giving *myself* actually mean? It should be the most challenging 'give'; the starting point. All other giving will involve the individual who is doing the giving, but it is easier to think of giving things rather than self. It is also less demanding and less threatening, but it is the starting point. What am I? That is what God wants, or that others

---

104. 2 Corinthians 6:1.
105. 1 Corinthians 12:27.
106. Luke 6:12-16; Luke 10:1.
107. John 1:12.

might need. We live in a world of busy-ness and pressure to be doing things – trying to justify our own existence. These things may not be bad in themselves, but can crowd out the better. So what does God actually want? The answer is really very simple, so simple that it may not look right, or enough. 'What does the LORD require of you? To act justly and to love mercy and to walk humbly with your God.'[108] This is beautiful.

It all starts with good living. A life that gives itself away in treating other people well and in relaxed relationship with God – a life of worship. Very much like the words of Jesus, '"Love the Lord your God with all your heart and with all your soul and with all your mind." This is the first and greatest commandment. And the second is like it: "Love your neighbour as yourself"',[109] again such obviously right-sounding words, but they actually demand everything.

Relationship with God starts with worship, a word that may automatically make us think 'church'. Wrong! Sure, that is where we often do it together, and should, but unless we learn to enjoy God alone, we are very limited. Our very reason for existence is 'to glorify God, and to enjoy him forever'.[110] So what is worship? It is about relationship, not primarily hymns, prayers, orders of service or sermons; it is about being with God and enjoying Him and the experience! How might we do that? It is not about rituals and routines, although developing good spiritual habits can help. Learn to make God part of your day, part of your normality. Learn to chat with Him about what you are doing and thinking; your plans and problems, people and

---

108. Micah 6:8.
109. Matthew 22:37-39.
110. Westminster Shorter Catechism, www.shortercatechism.com/resources/wsc/wsc_001.html (accessed 13 February 2023).

needs, opportunities and responsibilities. You can even laugh! Maybe cry. Read your Bible for pleasure, though this does not exclude a reading programme, if you have one. They can be very helpful.

Preferences, 'the way I like things' are not bad in themselves, but can be used badly. They are always a potential problem in worshipping together. The building, style, format, content, music, dress-code and interactions are all opportunities for friction! We are all different and that is good. We are God's children, but family life means different people *functioning together*! The challenge is to 'fit in' – blessed giving:

Each other's needs to prefer
For it is Christ we are serving[111]

Things start to fall into place as you share them. Actually, God is putting them in place! Being at one with God puts us in position to look beyond, to the other things we need to be doing, the being *fair, kind, loving*. Finding the right thing to do. Who needs me to make these things happen? How might that work out? Who needs my resources of time and availability? To talk and listen, to pray. to advise or assist? What 'things' do I have, to use, lend, or even give? Obviously that needs a responsible attitude – do not lend your car to somebody with no licence! Where can I sacrifice my preferences: 'I would rather be doing . . . but . . .' or my privileges: 'I don't have to do that/go there, but . . .' This is the Ministry of Inconvenience! God can do things through it that cannot be done any other way. And we gradually learn to like it!

---

111. 'The Servant King', Graham Kendrick Copyright © 1983 Thankyou Music.

Christian living is much more than philanthropy; it is a deliberate release of self, motivated by love and enabled by faith, an active policy of personal involvement and imaginative sharing. My main resource is what I am; what God has made me. It is unique, nobody else can be me, nobody else can give what I am. It is my spiritual worship and has limitless dimensions in the hand of God to become as big as it takes. What God has made, remade and is making in me (what I am) is the material for miracles – the place to multiply what is and to provide what isn't!

Chapter 7

Is My Giving Realistic?

'Giving' includes the whole of our resources, not just our money, but 'ourselves', all that we are and have, whatever that may mean. As we have seen, we are challenged to be givers, called to think and live in God-dimensions, expressing *agape/hesed* love. We are also very real humans – God has made us that way! If Christianity is not about reality, it is not about anything! As a result, we may be put in a position where we may have the potential for facing 'giving' situations, but with the fear of inadequacy, loss or restriction. The feelings of: 'Have I got enough? Can I afford to be a giver? If so, to what extent?' In theory, we know that all God's resources are available to us, as His agents, but do we place limits on our giving? We may (stupidly) start to think, 'Have I got access to His resource account? Might I become bankrupt? What is realistic? Is God realistic?' This is not a 'crisis of faith', it is about stopping to think and Jesus says it is OK! Look at His story of the man building a tower.[112] Could he afford to finish it? Should he stop building (at least, for the time being)? Common sense is part of what has been put into our being; it has its dangers. It is not a sin, but must not be allowed to become one by turning it into an excuse for not doing what God is

---

112. Luke 14:28.

saying. Sadly, our limits to common sense have often not come to terms with the promises of God. By nature, we prefer to play safe, to control the situation ourselves, but at what stage does caution become a lapse of faith – or blatant sin?

Is God really big enough (and interested enough) to meet all our needs? Are those 'needs' genuine?

Are there limits?

So, *are* there any limits to my love? Maybe not as far as desire is concerned; love is the hallmark of Christian living and has been from the beginning: 'By this everyone will know that you are my disciples, if you love one another.'[113] This has always challenged the world's thinking and still does. Real Christianity is very attractive. However, love is not stupid or naïve. Desire for doing 'nice things' has also to be put in realistic perspective. It may be very nice to give children sweets every time they ask; it may not be so nice taking them to the dentist later on! Good parents know when to say 'no'. By nature, we like more than necessities. Reaching towards degrees of luxury is a real temptation. Demands can be endless, but what are the actual needs in any given situation? Love sometimes needs to be tough and this may be misunderstood: 'Don't you want to help me'; 'Don't you care'?

Love has no limits, for God or us. We saw the example of Jesus in Philippians. He went all the way – '*even* death on a cross'.[114] Total love; nothing left. Our love needs to learn from Him, in attitude and in practice. The real question is, 'Do I want to go this way?' Humanly, the honest may be

---

113. John 13:35.
114. Philippians 2:8, emphasis mine.

'no'. But if, as a disciple, I say 'yes', what is the reason? Is it that I want to be seen as a 'super-saint'? That is pride and the answer is 'don't'. Or maybe it is to be able to relax into a perverted 'comfort' of acceptable behaviour in my particular Christian context, not to be bothered.

Do I really want to identify with Jesus in fulfilling *agape*; to be an effective agent in His world? Now we are getting somewhere and if we are being led into the way of obedience, that is what God wants. Obedient love can achieve remarkable things, because it has become a tool in the hand of God Himself. He can resource it. I can be a part in doing His miracles. Do I want that? Am I afraid? Might I be embarrassed? God does not want us to be unrealistic; He wants us to find new dimensions of what is possible, with His resources. To delight others and to amaze ourselves! It delights Him too.

Do we claim limits?

In defence of our frequent unwillingness to go the whole (or even part) way along this road, we may start to claim limits, to modify challenges:

a) 'The use of my resources is my choice.' That is true, but that does not automatically make it right. It needs also to see the place of obedience and responsibility in the opportunity that God is showing me.

b) 'What I am doing is reasonable.' ... 'As much as can be expected, as much as I can handle.' It is avoiding the reality of faith. This way I could make out a case for anything if I want to. That is the problem, what do I want? Can limits actually make me happy?

Jesus said, 'I delight to do Your will'.[115] The question for me is, 'Do I'?

c) 'I have already been quite generous.' How generous? Is it about staying within my comfort zone? Am I open to God's leading and opportunity to become bigger? Is my pseudo-safety actually worth having? Am I deluding myself? Am I trying to impress others?

d) 'It is more than they deserved.' Indeed, in some situations that may be true. It also raises the question, 'Does anybody deserve anything?' That opens the whole subject of 'rights'. In spite of the popular use of the word, the only person with genuine 'rights' is God, and He chooses not to use them! Jesus laid His down for us. He invites us to follow. The 'undeserving' person may desperately need what God has given me and that I could give to them.

e) 'Why should I?' If it is what God may be showing you (and the question is worth asking, as long as you are ready for an answer – He may not be!), then follow it through with Him.

f) 'It is unrealistic/not possible.' This may at present be true, or may be just another excuse. It may be the answer now, but may change. Do I want it to change? Would I rethink? God is the God of possibilities. What He actually asks is by definition possible! How, is another question.

There are always excuses (not 'reasons'), if we are unwilling to go that extra mile. The decision is ours and so are the

---

115. Psalm 40:8, NKJV.

outcomes. Remember, with real people in real situations, we are called to ask, 'Is this a place for the Transforming Principle?' If it is, remember that God has unlimited resources and that they are available for doing His will. 'The silver is mine and the gold is mine', and 'the cattle on a thousand hills'[116] (and with the price of beef being what it is, that is a lot!). I remember a friend saying, 'Where do you suppose He keeps it?' The answer is, usually 'in my bank account'! Do I *want* to be part of God's answer to this situation? How far am I willing to reach into my resources to achieve God's will?

What is God saying?

Is He really saying this, or have I got this idea from some other, possibly unreliable source? My response should be to follow what *God* is actually saying:

a) First, look at the 'need'. Be people-aware and open to the possibility of expressing appropriate practical love. Not all 'needs' are immediate, or even justified. Praying can bring focus to all sides of the situation. Not to talk God out of it, but to be open to the possibility of action. Pray in terms of 'show me what you want, Lord and I will do it'. If you really mean that, be ready for an answer!

b) Then assess the situation. Is it a one-off that needs relief, or something that needs long-term resolution? How urgent is it? Is it a matter for another resource – Social Services, 'the Church', or an appropriate charity? Or is it 'my baby'; within

---

116. Haggai 2:8; Psalm 50:10

my resources? Do not be afraid or embarrassed to explore and find what is possible.

c) Ask. Pray. Maybe consult for advice on how to proceed, but do so honestly. Sometimes we are wanting a reason *not* to proceed! If the answer is clear, volunteer. The resources may look very finite in the present; but in the will of God, it can multiply in His hands – remember the loaves and fishes.[117] I love Jesus' invitation to His disciples here – 'You give them something', and He meant it! There is another delightful turn in John's account – 'Here is a boy . . .'[118] God can involve anybody in giving.

d) Continue. How far, how long? Until you know it is time to stop, or change . . . Reassess. What is happening? Is it right? Are there any new factors? God gives us minds to think and imagine, to see possibilities. When it is right, God looks after the consequences of our obedience. But it can still be scary!

What about the 'other person?'

We are not called to do things *at* people, they need to be involved in the 'answer' too, particularly in the longer-term. Trying to prevent the situation from recurring and also, at least in part, paying back, when that is appropriate. It will help their personal dignity if they are able to contribute. Explain what you are trying to do. Personal accountability will help to discourage parasitism; a real danger in those who habitually go the same wrong ways.

---

117. Matthew 14:15-21.
118. John 6:9.

The aim should be not only to relieve, but to rehabilitate; finding better ways to live and, best of all, to find new life in Christ and complete the solution. New people who can discover transformed living to share with others, growing themselves and then becoming givers. They will understand the problems of similar people.

Underlying questions

Ask yourself: 'What resources do I have available to use in helping?' The obvious one that many people are asking for is money! Throwing money at a situation will often provide a short-term relief. It is, in that sense, easy. It may avoid the sweat and tears of giving more than money. God calls us to engage with the people in the situation. Time, availability, praying and pastoral input are all much better investments. Humans are spiritual beings; spiritual weakness through unbelief or sin needs to be met with spiritual answers. The added spiritual resources of other people, too, may in the long-term be very important.

Maybe a lot of this is very obvious. One of the biggest questions is when to say 'no' to habitual graspers! God does not call us to be unwise, and later He may show more clearly what He is saying. If uncertain, it is better to err on the side of generosity – with continuing assessment of the situation. God looks at our motives, as well as those of the other person!

Most of what I have been saying is about people-problems. Often people turn up at the door of churches, perhaps with a tale of woe, often incomplete or even untrue. God's way is not to simply 'get rid of them'. Christians can be very gullible, for the best of reasons, but love is called even to give to the undeserving, even when we know it. God can take what we offer and do with it more than we can imagine. Realistic but caring firmness is often needed to try to bring structure to these problems. People in addiction in particular may need careful handling. We may find that confrontation is not a contradiction to compassion. They need to find a better way; the right way. In some circumstances, we may ask, what can be done when genuine effort is not being effective? A positive discontinuing of the help that has already been given, with an explanation, but not withdrawing from praying, or contact may be needed.

In the end, real, effective answers may need long-term help, and we need wisdom around what to give, when to give, and how to proceed when the situation is a difficult one. So, giving is realistic – but we need discernment!

Chapter 8

The 'M'-word

It had to come! We have seen already (and will see more), that 'giving' covers many areas of Christian living and ministry, but the recurring regular one meets us every Sunday morning when it is time for the 'Offering'! 'Collection' is a rather heartless term, more about method than meaning. Many Christians now do their giving online, or by Direct Debit, but there is value in making it part of our worship in a more visible way – a tangible act of worship. That has been so for thousands of years in biblical history, through to today.

Most of us now live in non-agricultural communities, but even for those who do, chickens, bags of grain do not fit with normal church life! So that means money! Talking about financial transactions does not look very 'spiritual'. It has always aroused negative feelings and comments from those who do not understand the importance and validity of giving, but the Transforming Principle also applies clearly to that part of our lives. It is a positive and important Bible theme, dating from God's instructions in the Old Testament and developed by Jesus' critiquing of what was happening in His day and St Paul's extension of this in the spreading Church. It is a realistic, practical and very valid part of worship – recognising and thanking God for providing for our livelihood and beyond – 'life and breath and everything'.[119]

A continuing theme is that of proportionality – the 'tithe', one-tenth of all income. The danger with that is that it can become a hard-nosed mathematical exercise, which stops as soon as you have 'done your bit'! Giving becomes just a slot in a programme and not an integral part of life itself.

Another temptation is to manipulate the figures to look good, to avoid any real challenge! There is no stimulus to living by real faith. The tithe was augmented by many other times and types of giving – for specific thanks events, special needs and for a desire to 'do more', as God stimulates thinking to see what He sees; 'vision' that we could resource and see happen. There are many possibilities for giving. It is an important part of Christian living.

Inevitably, anything to do with money is open to criticism – just or unjust. The Church is often seen as 'after your money' – and sadly, the behaviour of some churches can be seen to justify this! We need to get beyond the negativity and sometimes dishonesty, into realistic and generous giving, which thanks God for what we have and that He can 'bless'.

We all like receiving and the security (and even status) that it gives, but we need constantly to remember that the ultimate origin of this is God Himself – the great Giver. Is He 'blessed' by doing this? Not by most people – they do not look far enough back and see income only as a due reward for work. We can bless Him for all He gives. We call it worship: 'Bless the LORD, O my soul'.[120]

---

119. Acts 17:25.
120. Psalm 103, NKJV.

What then, can be our identifiable giving, in which we can be blessed? We have other definable resources than money, such as time, also abilities and usable assets, but we are concentrating on 'the big one'!

Income

That may affect each of us differently:

Paid Employment. This is a major factor. It is clearly identifiable (including by the tax man!) and should be realistically defined and directed in our Christian giving. Interestingly and importantly in the origins of tithing, the 10 per cent was only a starting point![121] There were many other offerings of a non-mathematical origin, given 'from the heart'. This should still be so. A way of saying 'thank you'.

For those with higher incomes, what should be done? 10 per cent could be derisory! Ask God and see what He says – you will probably already have a good idea! The answer may even be 50 per cent, or more . . . Maybe not on a Sunday morning, but through the year. Actually, we should be prepared to give 100 per cent. Jesus said, 'Those of you who do not give up everything . . . cannot be my disciples'[122] – everything we have should be totally available to God. After all, where did it come from in the first place? In Genesis 1:29-31 it was God who gave, and He did it again at Calvary. God does not get giving wrong; we are the ones that run into trouble, misusing His trust in us; Adam and Eve got it wrong. We continue to do it too!

If there is no 'cost' to giving (i.e. no challenge to our inner being), godly rethinking needs to be done. Does that

---

121. See Malachi 3:10.
122. Luke 14:33.

mean that we should only feel 'right' when under continual stress? God does not want to kill us! He has His ways of encouraging and affirming.

I still clearly remember many years ago of responding to a major challenge to give. I even knew how much and the following Sunday, gave a four-figure sum for the first time. This did not come 'out of nowhere'. For many years I had been a regular giver – tithing was not new to me, but it was somewhat of a routine. Finances were tight and I was not very well-paid. I was rather apprehensive . . . Amazingly, in the post on Monday was an unexpected cheque for three times what I had given! God has His ways. Let me hasten to add, that it has not happened again! It is not a reason to try to 'bribe' God. He wants us to be secure in Him, not to walk a financial tightrope.

Limited Employment. For those not in regular, or full-time work (such as when I was a student, doing holiday jobs to stay solvent; and other types of less regular employment), a course to recommend is:

Desire to give – from what you have. Pray and ask 'what'? 'Be . . . convinced in [your] own mind'.[123] This may not be just financial. What else do you have that could be given, or used?

Decide to give – be deliberate about what you know is right; you *will* know! 'Give what you have decided in your heart to give, not reluctantly or under compulsion'[124]

Do it! Make a start. Not ridiculously, but with an intention to increase. It will change over time, as your circumstances change. God will help you to get it right.

---

123. Romans 14:5.
124. 2 Corinthians 9:7.

Update. As things change. Never stop updating. Keep your giving under review.

Part-time Employment is a necessity for many people whose 'other commitments' – particularly in families with young children, when a parent has to work to 'make ends meet'. It will probably change with time as the children get more self-sufficient. This is a perfectly valid 'double duty', but the income actually derived should be considered as part of the parental personal commitment to giving.

Family Giving. Young people of 'giving age' (i.e. some sort of 'income', even 'pocket money') should work out their own commitment to giving as Christians, but couples (with or without dependent children) should ideally resolve their giving together, based on their combined income. This is a time of household commitment as a whole, as well as their church giving (and to other causes). These are best done as a mutual decision, or there may well be confusion, or even animosity, self-interest or dishonesty. Not a good thing for the family!

Christian families often have special and important opportunities for 'blessed giving', particularly in family ministry together – such as the 'Ministry of Hospitality' – an important Bible theme.[125] 'Some people have shown hospitality to angels without knowing it'![126]

Money!

Worldwide, some sort of tangible assets are used. Increasingly we are getting a 'cashless society'. Electronic banking is seeing a sharp decrease in cheque use, as well

125. Romans 12:13.
126. Hebrews 13:2.

as hard cash. In whatever form, money has challenged God's people throughout history. It brings its own set of problems:

Security. There is something comforting to know that we have no problems! This is actually a danger – it can become a replacement for faith, but 'life does not consist in an abundance of possessions'.[127] In Luke 12:13-21, Jesus told a story about a man who did very well. He sat back to enjoy life with no stress, but did not realise he was in great danger. He would die that night! The reverse problem is stupidity and irresponsibility: 'God will look after me.' Yes, He may do, but with appropriate discipline.

Dishonesty. How much is 'enough'? How can I make it bigger? This desire can escalate and end up in big trouble as the desire starts to use increasingly suspect methods. 'The love of money is a root of all kinds of evil.'[128] We see it all the time! It is the 'love' that is the sin, not the money. Money is a useful servant, but a very bad master – it can drive us into things that are plain wrong – even into gaol!

Wilting Faith. Easy living is risky living. It slowly pushes our loving God aside: 'I don't need actually Him any more.' We may still go to church, still call ourselves Christians, still support charities, but the pressure is off. We have lost the cutting edge.

Somebody once said that the last part of ourselves to be converted is our wallet (or our bank account)! Christian giving affects our whole being, but the 'M-word' remains an ongoing challenge, whatever stage we are at.

---

127. Luke 12:15.
128. 1 Timothy 6:10.

If we do not face it early, it will become increasingly difficult, and the larger our income and resources become, the more difficult it is to give positively and realistically. 'Trivial' expenditure on things like cars or holidays can be done almost without thinking. When it comes to planned, regular commitment to realistic giving, we need to continue in deliberate sacrifice. Blessed giving is not about trivia, it is about the kingdom of God. That needs motivation to question and assess the true depth of how we are giving – 'your kingdom come, your will be done, on earth!'[129] Where am I here and now?

'Money' should not be a dirty word; it should be what I am managing well – in God's full view. Can I say truthfully 'I delight to do Your will' – whatever it costs?

---

129. Matthew 6:10.

79

Chapter 9

The Cost of Giving

The key to effective ministry is giving – what we put into it, willingly and positively. That means that the full range of our resources (not just financial) is always available for God to use. It transforms the giver and also what God is calling them to do. It is our mission to fulfil; now and lifelong. It is not about bravado or pseudo-spiritual masochism, which would be a childish exhibitionism of false commitment; an attempt (even if incidental) of magnifying our own ministry, rather than that of the One who calls. Nor is it bribery: 'Look what I have done, Lord, I expect you to bless it – and me!' God does not ask or want us to try to impress anybody, particularly Himself. He knows our motives already. 'God loves a cheerful giver',[130] not a devious one!

Whose ministry is it anyway, and why are we doing it? God calls us to be His agents in His world, indeed, the universe! His call to us is initially to discipleship: followers, learners – an expanding experience. The initial call can come to us any age and is often multiple and always sequential; learners are always finding more and better. They are perpetual students. That is one of our delightful surprises, you can never outgrow God. God always has more and is waiting to extend Himself to us as we move

---

130. 2 Corinthians 9:7.

on. We need to have a progressing mentality, so we are ready for Him to speak. We need to be stopping to ask, 'Lord, what do you want me to do?' When He shows us, the only appropriate response is: 'Yes!'

The call to faith can (and usually does) come in many ways: by 'hearing . . . the word about Christ.'[131] That may have been preached (often), read (in the Bible, or other books), told to us, or even found incidentally – picked up somewhere in the passage of life. God is a comprehensive Communicator. Often faith comes through observation – seeing the real thing in action, maybe over many years. This provokes questions in the observer's mind. 'These people are different, why?' And here is a challenge to every Christian, as to the quality of what we say we believe and how we live it. We do not want a 'Ministry of Disappointment'.

Discipleship works through similar channels. Those who followed Jesus heard his teaching, digested it and then saw it in action – a practical demonstration for them to copy. There was a huge and comprehensive variety to absorb. What would happen next? Jesus was full of surprises. He kept on calling them onwards in their experiences and service.

At the end of His course, when Jesus returned to heaven, He commanded them to continue His ministry, but expanded the scope from Palestine to the world. He passed on the same methodology to them 'go . . . make disciples . . . baptising them . . . teaching them [to do the same]'.[132] It has continued throughout history and is still relevant. He said 'go', and they went. Paul was a second-generation disciple,

131. Romans 10:17.
132. Matthew 28:19-20.

called by direct verbal intervention from heaven, and then sent into the world at large by another call at his church in Antioch.[133] This happened in the context of 'normal' church life. Is my church like that? He became the most travelled of all the apostles; no obstacle was too much. He it was who passed on the fruit of the Transforming Principle to the Mediterranean world and then into Europe. This was his motivating force and he saw it as of universal application. Time and again he paid for his obedience to it, in many physical, emotional and spiritual traumas, eventually paying the same price as his Master, though (probably) in the Colosseum at Rome, not on a cross.

For many, the cost is 'too much' – financially, professionally, or personally. David got it right: should he give to God that which cost him nothing?[134] Trying to find cheap way round (not just financially) is a recipe for disaster; it doesn't work! God does not play half-measures; obedience has no shortcuts. God looks after the consequences of our obedience: 'Seek first the kingdom of heaven . . . all the necessities will be added.'[135]

The scope of apostolic ministry was hinted at by Jesus in John 14:12: 'whoever believes in me will do the works I have been doing, and they will do even greater things . . .' Greater in number or in nature, or both? What is it that Jesus was doing? Preaching, teaching and healing – of body, mind and spirit. We sometimes get cold feet about this teaching, even more so when we find: '. . . drive out demons . . . speak in new tongues . . . pick up snakes . . . drink deadly poison' and heal the sick . . .'[136] This is the finishing piece

133. Acts 9:3-4; Acts 13:2.
134. 2 Samuel 24:24.
135. See Matthew 6:33.
136. Mark 16:17-18.

of Mark's Gospel and is not accepted by all. It is, however, still there. It means something! Do not belittle the teaching of Jesus, it is big. He does not call us to triviality; faith is always a challenge! It will cost us all that we are and all that we have, but the outcome will be amazing. Luke also concludes his Gospel with similar words: '. . . repentance for the forgiveness of sins will preached in [Jesus'] name to all nations . . . You are witnesses',[137] and so it happened. The worldwide Church stands as evidence to this day. The command to 'go' was passed on, and still is. It all started happening at Pentecost and the same Holy Spirit is still the same motivating power of God, as we get up, go out and give. *If* we go out and give! Why are we often so selective in our obedience? We are (moderately) happy to preach this message, but going is often a problem. As for the other things . . . What holds us back? Uncertainty, or its big brother, unbelief? Often it is fear, but of what? Misunderstanding, criticism (or frank ridicule), failure (I don't like egg on my face), vague bad reports from the past? There is fear in trying again. Part of the cost of being a giver is that we will take on 'the offence of the cross',[138] the risk of upsetting people, or even sadder, when the offended people call themselves Christians. So, where and what may that mean for us now?

Going. Where? The call of Paul and Barnabas happened in the normality of Church one Sunday! The Holy Spirit spoke into their worship, 'Set apart for me Barnabas and Saul . . . So . . . they . . . sent them off.'[139] What would that mean? Leaving home and a very 'good' church and their

---

137. Luke 24:47-48.
138. Galatians 5:11.
139. Acts 13:3.

very successful ministries there, then sailing for Cyprus and beyond. They knew not where. The rest is history; world mission had become a reality for the first time.

The opportunities for 'career missionaries' are very limited in some countries now, but on a shorter-term basis, with defined objectives, there are more possibilities than ever. Teaching, medicine and engineering are examples. I found myself in Romania twenty-five years ago for a surgical conference – a purely secular, university event. Little did I know, but I was aware of a clear desire to go back, initially on the same basis. A telephone call came three months later . . . Then came church connections, leading three teams from my own church and repeated visits for youth camps and other events. There continues to be a 'rightness' to it. God has his ways! And there have also been times of great disappointment and pain; I have been learning the cost of being a giver. However, ultimately it has done me no harm. God calls us into joy, but not always fun.

Giving. Sometimes the call to involvement is in the practicalities of enabling others to follow their call. Finance is an eminently practical way of doing this. It should not be an avoidance of the possibility of going personally, and entails the responsibility of possible continuing interest, praying and encouragement for those who do. It can be a very good way of ministry by involvement for those who are prevented from actually going for physical or other reasons. We are all called to world concern and can all do it, though our opportunities and methods will be different.

A warning. Look at whatever ministry you have, or aspire to. Have you actually been called to it? By whom? How?

How was it confirmed? We need to face the possibility that we may be on an ego trip; something that sounds good, impresses others or makes us feel good – even superior. What we are doing may seem to be very 'successful', or even spectacular. It may be very 'costly', but that does not confirm it. What is our real motivation? Maybe self-justification with God – a sort of spiritual bribery for His favour. We need to be doing the right thing for the right reason. Both are important. Poor motives lead eventually to poor outcomes – personally, in terms of genuine satisfaction and practically, in spiritual depth.

It has been said that evangelism exists to answer the questions raised by our worship. This certainly applies to our Sundays (which sadly may not raise many questions!). What do our churches express to their neighbours and community? How well do we engage in local issues and opportunities? The whole of our lives should be worship – an offering to glorify God. Yes, there is a cost in doing God's will and He does not want us to be unrealistic. Faith is not stupidity. Nor is it not daunted by challenge, but desirous to see it happen. So, what are our lives saying to God, to each other and to outsiders? Does a 'giving mentality' define what I am doing? What is that saying, and to whom? Am I at risk of growing satisfied – even smug – with what I have done? Am I awake and seeking whatever God may have in His mind?

Chapter 10

The Touch of Death!

The early Church were amazingly supportive of one another[140] – possibly unwisely at times. Ananias and Sapphira famously fiddled the system, with disastrous results.[141] Try to imagine this scenario . . .

You are with a group of friends, doing whatever friends do. One of them says to you, 'Remember that money you lent me? I can pay it back now.' And he hands you the money. One of the others then says (one who you have lent to before and who has not paid back), 'Oh, I could do with that, could you lend it to me, please?' I have seen it happen! So there you are with the money in your hand and an unresolved problem from the past. How do you feel and what does your hand do? I suspect that your immediate reaction is a negative one and your hand closes on the money. This may not be the end of the story. More needs to happen before the hand can open. Has there been habitual asking? Has there been any lying, cheating or illegality? A firm reply may be needed, probably with caveats and 'suggestions'. There needs to be a distinction between naivety, or even complicity. Unresolved problems from the past may need 'tough love'. Refusal, with explanation and suggestions, may be the right course.

---

140. Acts 4:32-35.
141. Acts 5:1-11.

When it comes to giving and receiving, what do our hands 'say'? With receiving, they are happy and open, but with giving (particularly doubtful giving), they close. But, if they are personally trying to retain, they become clenched tightly. Our hands match our feelings; relaxed, or tense and anxious. Our hands mirror our lives.

God's call on our lives is to give away our faith, that is evangelism, and to give away ourselves in the process, in pastoral care and practical love. To reach out to others (sometimes literally) with openness to help, by passing on to them the blessings of God to us that they need, so that they find the reality of new life. We also find the strength and resources to live it, so that they can then move forward into a new and better future. That means opening our 'hands', both literally and figuratively. As we have just seen, that may pose problems for us! Being firm but fair may well involve pastoral care. This is also giving!

The hands that are open are in the position to give; they are also in the position to receive more, of what? And then what?

More of everything from the God who gives everything. Resources to live and to give.

More to enjoy! Don't feel guilty about enjoying what God gives – He likes making people happy! More to pass on – to deploy, to do the work He gives us to do; it should also be a good experience. He wants us to be like Him, enjoying blessing others. The open hand that has just given can then be laid on the recipient as an expression of goodwill and blessing.

If we decide to retain what *could* be given (for whatever reason), our hands close and things happen in our minds. We may retain to have pleasure in the security of 'having'. Maybe even with a feeling of smug satisfaction! We don't feel reduced in our resources and maybe even have a sense of pride. 'I am alright.' These are dangerous attitudes; they have consequences:

Firstly, closed hands cannot receive any more and God is always wanting to give, so that we will become bigger and thus able to do better. The closed hands get tighter and a (right) sense of guilt will worsen this. Try this practical demonstration ... Clench your fists and keep them clenched. Don't relax, keep them that way for a few minutes. Keep going, don't let go! Now, what are you feeling? Pain! Now let go. Relief! Deliberate retaining of God's good gifts starts to hurt us. We are not happy. Our minds focus on the pain and lose sight of the blessing. We need to learn to hold things lightly, so they can grow, be released and explode into unexpected release and blessing!

The **Second** consequence of refusing to let go is that the clenched fist slowly crushes what it is holding. When we eventually relax to enjoy what we are holding for ourselves, even to gloat over what we have, we may well find that there is nothing left. We have killed it. Or maybe there are just the shrivelled remains of a good gift. The pathetic ghost of what was; a sick memory. And we are left angry, grieving over what was and what might have been. Giving hands are happy hands, blessed into continued action with more receiving and blessing. Greedy hands can never be truly happy; they are uncomfortable and actually useless.

Selfishness is a sin; indeed, it is the basis of all sin. We see it again and again, just as at the Fall – it comes in inexorable stages:

- I **like**. The selfish attraction of even good things, even 'right' things, generates thoughts of more. Our motives have become corrupted.

- I **want**. The 'thing' may not be bad or 'wrong', but what is my motivation for wanting it? Is it just because I want to be bigger, more important, more 'used' (getting dangerous now): 'after desire has conceived, it gives birth to sin'[142] and a lot of spiritual injury in the short term.

- I **will**. The final step; taking, regardless of what I know is right: 'sin, when it is full-grown, gives birth to death'[143] and a lot of spiritual injury in the short term.

Sin is always corrupting – it spoils everything it touches, leaving a stinking mess! Can you smell anything in your life? Is something bad oozing out?

Sin is also destructive, it kills the sinner; it has its pay-off *'the wages of sin is death'*[144] and it kills the effectiveness of the Christian.

Jesus gave another working principle, also an expression of the Transforming one: 'Those who save, lose; those who lose, saves.'[145]

Is it 'wrong' to receive? An important question, before you go on a guilt trip! If God is the great Giver, who does He give to and why? If He is so generous to everybody, how should we relate to that? Should we be asking Him not to give, so we do not feel guilty? The answer is obviously 'no', so where are we? To be looking to receive, *as an aim*, is the problem. If we are just looking to Him for more all the time, it is a form of religious greed. He calls us to be Team with Him and that needs resources; the job is too big for human abilities and resources alone. Kingdom work needs

---

142. James 1:15.
143. James 1:15.
144. Romans 6:23.
145. See Matthew 10:39.

kingdom resources and kingdom commitment. The King is there to deliver the necessary, the Team is there to deploy the results – 'workers together with Him'.[146] Receiving as a result of what we are doing is different; more like wages – an outcome of our serving; the consequences being bigger resources that can be recycled into serving, so we can do more and better.

Matthew 7:11 tells us that God delights to give good gifts to His children, so don't be embarrassed! Be thankful, then ask constructive questions, like 'why and what'? We may not know at present, but the use for the gift will become evident later. Not that need is the only reason God gives. He loves to give; He is an encourager. Maybe we have got something right! And we should be delighted too, not ungrateful and certainly not just asking 'pseudo-holy questions'! So, receive, you have been honoured and respected – 'Well done, good and faithful servant . . . Enter into the joy of your lord.'[147] He can trust you with even more delight as you succeed in His work with what He is giving, overflowing in grace, with the grace you have been given.

Not to overflow is the mistake. 'Collecting' grace is misuse of it! It has many negative effects, some of them not very beautiful. Lazy 'faith', overweight and overloaded religious obesity, which makes us ugly and useless. Spiritual constipation is another unpleasant disease; overfull and unable to clear ourselves for pleasanter work! A slightly more polite problem is loss of our spiritual cutting edge – blunt and inefficient. We become restricted in our service through misappropriated gifts. The bottom line? No joy! And worse, God's disapproval and disappointment; we

---

146. 2 Corinthians 6:1, NKJV.
147. Matthew 25:21, NKJV.

bring Him no joy either. The world laughs! They always suspected that we were frauds. And Satan laughs too! We have been doing his work for him.

There has been a lot of negativity in this chapter, but getting our lives wrong, particularly as Christians, is a no-win situation. If that is where your life or mine is going, it needs urgent action. What?

Is it time to confess? To be straight with God and admit the problem, the sin, the neglect, the wrong motives? Then, after some honesty, it is time to repent, the Greek *metanoia,* a change of mind; a decision to put things right. Then something wonderful can happen. God releases us 'If we confess our sins, he is faithful and just and will forgive us our sins and purify us'[148] and gives us a new start, space to get life right again. To relax. To come back to Life.

---

148. 1 John 1:9.

Chapter 11

Bad News or Good News?

The nature of sacrifice

The word 'sacrifice' produces immediate negative reactions in our thinking. It raises images of gruesome rites in primitive cultures. It is, however, a strong word in the Bible, particularly in the Old Testament, where it has very clear meaning and applications. It needs, therefore, to be defined in four general concepts:

- Of what? Historically and culturally, there are religious rules about this. The sacrifice often involves, animals, even humans, but also of agricultural (or other) produce, or valuables. It is deliberate and intentional.
- To what? Usually a deity, but it can be to another person.
- By whom? The donor, who bears the cost. It is about giving, not lending.
- For what? To achieve a purpose, such as forgiveness, or placation, or for life – needs, like rain, fertility, crops. It may also express gratitude.

The word is often trivialised, usually to refer to some sort of discomfort in life, to achieve an end, or make a point. This is a misnomer and is more like an 'investment'. We give, so we can get. There is an 'agenda', even though it may not happen. This is not what we are talking about, and which may end up very *un*-blessed!

The New Testament is based on a sacrifice already made by Jesus Christ – the 'Lamb of God'[149] – who died for our sins.[150] This fitted closely with a pattern already laid down in the Old Testament. Is that, then, the end of sacrifice? No! St Paul wrote of the importance of sacrifice, a breath-taking doxology to the grace of God, concluding with, 'For from him and through him and for him are all things. To him be the glory for ever! Amen.'[151] 'He then moves into the subject of an appropriate response, 'Therefore . . . in view of God's mercy . . . offer your bodies as a living sacrifice . . . this is your appropriate worship.'[152] Our bodies express the real 'us' – all we are and have. Sacrifice and worship are very closely related concepts for Christians. Both are about making an appropriate response to who God is and what He has done for us – individually and corporately. They are about giving ourselves and our resources into serving Him in the context of the needs and opportunities of where we are – being His agents of 'salvation'. That means an appropriate release of resources.

The Old Testament is full of sacrifices for different situations, and those for sin involved the giving of a life. To our way of thinking, they were messy and repugnant, but they expressed the seriousness of sin. Sin is not a vague abstract noun – it is rebellion against the good and right ways of a loving and caring God, though often that rebellion seems to come from nowhere! We seem by nature to be

149. John 1:29.
150. 1 Peter 3:18.
151. Romans 11:36.
152. Romans 12:1.

warped to choose the wrong thing, to behave as if we are the god of our own destiny. The 'Original Temptation' was 'you will be like God',[153] and the sin was in stepping past Him into what had been explicitly forbidden. 'The rest', as they say, 'is history', and is still very much with us. The biggest problem for every person in the world is: 'What can I do with my sin?' It was a problem for God too! He cannot pretend it is not there, or that it does not matter. Some sort of 'punishment' is appropriate, but so is His desire to do something to resolve the issue. Killing the offender may solve one problem, but would immediately make another – what would become of the guilty human race? The short-term answer started with the death of an animal – to clothe the naked and ashamed Adam and Eve.[154] God provides!

By the time of the Exodus, the concept became more defined. The Passover[155] became both a judgement (on the offending Egyptians) and a salvation (for the participating Jews) through the blood of a sacrificial lamb; faith expressed in obedience, as defined by God. Much more comprehensive worship and sacrifice soon followed by the constructing of the Tabernacle and later of the Temple. But how could the death of an animal achieve forgiveness for a guilty human? The simple answer is, it can't! The writer to the Hebrews faced this fact: 'The law is only a shadow ... sacrifices [can never] make perfect ... It is impossible for the blood of bulls and goats to take away sins.'[156]

So, what then? 'When Christ came into the world, he said: ... "a body you prepared for me"'; 'I desire to do your will'.[157] The whole of the past system had pointed to a final

---

153. Genesis 3:5.
154. Genesis 3:21.
155. Exodus 12:12-13.
156. Hebrews 10:1-4.
157. Hebrews 10:5; Psalm 40:8.

sacrifice – of Jesus Christ. God had provided the 'Lamb' from Himself and for Himself. He personally 'paid the bill' for our forgiveness. What follows?

We have seen many examples of sacrifice already and by nature, we do not like doing it – even when we are called to. Sacrifice is unpleasant and costly. It challenges our attempts at self-sufficiency, but God asks for our whole being, not just the convenient and disposable parts of our lives. As you have been reading, where have you been nudged to think seriously about giving? Over the years of Christian experience, where have you faced these issues? What did you do? What happened?

Our first expression of sacrifice probably comes with conversion, the humiliation of admitting there is a problem – facing the reality of our sin and the necessity of salvation. Repentance is an admission of failure, a change of thinking and a desire to do something – saying 'yes' to what God has done for us in Jesus. This is a 'compulsory' chain of events, which may cause initial apprehensions! 'Am I being stupid?' 'What might happen?' 'What might people say?' 'Can I keep it up?'

The atonement for our sin by Jesus was a horrendous event, but how did He face it? 'For the joy that was set before him he endured the cross'.[158] Joy? Yes, because He knew the outcome – it was His destiny; why He had come into the world. Humanly, His last hours looked like a dark and threatening disaster 'overwhelmed with sorrow', but He faced them in total obedience and submission – 'not as I will, but as you will'.[159] The prospect of the cross appalled Him, but He did not divert from this ultimate giving. He had

---

158. Hebrews 12:2.
159. Matthew 26:38; Matthew 26:39.

already made the sacrifice; indeed, it had been 'from the beginning of time. This was before there was a problem!

Our call to sacrifice, like Jesus, is also in terms of obedience and commitment to what God is asking of us. In broad terms, that means giving ourselves into participating in His work in the world, in the situations and opportunities in which He places us. Blood sacrifice for forgiveness of sin has been made obsolete since Jesus died and has no longer been practised, even in Judaism, since the destruction of the Temple in AD70. The other types of sacrifice – freewill and thank offerings are always relevant. 'Tithes', as a clear 10 per cent of whatever 'income' means, are now given over into our own sense of responsibility: 'Each of you should give what you have decided in your heart'.[160] It is not imposed and indeed, 10 per cent may realistically be far too little! We are free to respond to the goodness of God and to express this in doing it. We can share the mindset of Jesus. This is in sacrificing ourselves to Him and likewise in discovering delight! We can follow Him in submission, sacrifice and then into new life and indeed, eventually into resurrection!

Sacrifice and worship are very closely related concepts for Christians. They are both about making an appropriate personal response to who God is and what He has done for us – individually and together. They are about giving ourselves and our resources into serving God in the needs and opportunities of where we are; being agents of 'salvation', whatever that needs to mean! We step out, not into a 'mistaken impossibility', but into amazing reality!

Our 'old' thinking is often tempted to find an easier way; to hold onto what we have – what we can see and feel.

---

160. 2 Corinthians 9:7.

We fall into the current thinking of 'risk assessment' and 'damage limitation'! We looked at this earlier, in Chapter 10, but let's think further about the problems of holding on . . .

The three pains of the grasping hand

Avoiding the way of sacrificial giving has complex consequences:

Physically – the tight grasp of saying 'no' to God's way and will is, in the immediate situation uncomfortable, even painful; an awareness that things are not right. In the longer-term, we lose the ability to function – we cannot do what we should be doing. Worse follows. The grasping hand becomes deformed and disabled.

Mentally – Function and objectivity become overpowered by refusal to release ourselves:

- Intellectually, we lose the ability to understand God. Our spiritual focus is diverted by self-justification, to try to find excuses for our actions. Then, our perception of what God is wanting becomes limited and unable to see the significance and value of *'His good, pleasing and perfect will.'*[161] We can only see negatives!

- Emotionally – frustration comes, as we choose to limit our response to God's way and fear mounts, as our chosen way is not 'working out'.

- Our will – to decide and do what is right shrinks into closed thinking, frustration and retreat into more indecision, whether to continue into failure, or to move back into repentance.

---

161. Romans 12:2.

Spiritually, we slip further out of harmony with God, into selfishness and separation. Everything in our being has become injured – possibly (maybe in part) permanently. Injured, but not destroyed – God still loves and cares even for 'bad' Christians. We have been deceived into thinking that generosity is profligacy and that sacrifice is stupidity. The 'father of lies'[162] is always trying to divert and destroy the work of God. Is there a way out of all this? Yes:

Wake up! As you become aware of where your life of faith has drifted, do something. Pray! The way of repentance and forgiveness is still open. 'If we confess our sins [God] ... will forgive ... and purify us' from whatever![163] This was written to Christians!

It is not a magic formula, but an ongoing opportunity. Be real with yourself. Be real with God. *Seek help.* Who could you talk with/pray with? Do it!

---

162. John 8:44.
163. 1 John 1:9.

99

Chapter 12

Living Like God

'God is love'[164] – overflowing *agape*. The Trinity – Father, Son and Holy Spirit – lives in continuous eternal relationship, as One God, described in ancient times as *perichoresis*, a dancing together in interactive enjoyment. He also calls Himself 'I AM',[165] a title that Jesus used many times, of Himself! The God who 'is', not defined by time and living outside it in an eternal present. As 'I am', God is always there and always the same, but not in a boring way and not fully predictable by humans, even Christians! Unlike God, time limits us; we are stuck with it and in it, but already we are living in eternal dimensions. Eternal life has started already and we are certainly not stuck *in* it! Experiencing it is to grow all the time. This tension between living in 'the now and the not yet' is a problem for us, but not for God. In us, it can sometimes generate feelings of frustration in the present and uncertainty in understanding the future: 'How long, LORD?'[166]

The unselfish fellowship of the Trinity desires to share what it has and is. It has always done so internally, but it has not always done so externally, so God created the universe

---

164. 1 John 4:8.
165. Exodus 3:14.
166. Psalm 13:1.

101

– with at least one inhabited planet, earth, the only one that we know about. It is as if he wanted a place where other beings could enjoy interactive Divine fellowship too. So, He has been at work:

From creation, when He brought everything that is into existence. How is another question, but to say that He did it *ex nihilo*, 'out of nothing', is to my scientific training, a nonsense. I think Albert Einstein helps us here; his Theory of Relativity – expressed as $E=mc^2$ – points to the interchangeability of mass (m), substance and energy (E), which is how the atomic bomb works! The reverse can apply. God, as the source of infinite energy, can thus produce mass ('stuff') out of Himself. He could then give Himself further into developing it. The account of God doing this in the opening of Genesis 1:1 shows His Name to be a Hebrew plural form; two or more – a Trinity. Having begun, the God who 'is', works on into . . .

The continuing 'Now'. As we saw earlier, He gives us 'life and breath and everything',[167] all that is needed to originate, sustain and enable our lives. St Paul points out that this involves Jesus, the Christ. He 'is the image of the invisible God . . . in him all things were created . . . in him all things hold together'.[168] He is much bigger than just 'our Saviour'; we are safe in Divine hands. He is the loving provider of everything, even for those who reject Him. This is what is called 'Common Grace'; all the good things that God provides for all people and which Paul explored when he visited pagan Athens, as we read in Acts 17. There

167. Acts 17:25.
168. Colossians 1:15-17.

were temples everywhere – plenty of religion, but little or no knowledge of God. His Jewish background gave him no common ground for spiritual discussion, until he noticed one temple dedicated to the 'UNKNOWN GOD'. The very one that Paul wanted to share with them? He started by quoting two of their own poets: 'In him we live and move and have our being'; indeed, 'We are his offspring.' God brought us into being and enables us in our living – 'He gives us life and breath and everything'.[169] He goes on to point out that this generous God also has expectations of us, and then made his way into presenting the challenge of the resurrected Jesus.

As we have already seen, Jesus spoke of the Father who provides even for birds and flowers and that we are of more value than they.[170] Later, Paul wrote of Jesus' part as Creator and Sustainer of all things – 'in him all things hold together'.[171] This is a helpful concept in looking at resources and their origins. Atheistic philosophy, if pushed repeatedly with the question 'Where did that come from?' will usually go back to the 'Big Bang'. All very well, but what went 'bang' and where did it come from? The call of Jesus is very much more about 'feet on the ground': 'Come to me', 'follow me', 'learn from me'[172] and then find new life. This was all initially physical, but later was given new and greater dimensions, both in nature and duration – the physical had become spiritual as well. It was to be linked in with the life of the eternal and all-giving God.

Just as humankind was called into being at creation, now Jesus continues to call into new being. He is the

169. Acts 17:22-28.
170. Matthew 6:26.
171. Colossians 1:17.
172. Matthew 11:28; Matthew 4:19; Matthew 11:29.

Giver of life, initially biological and then now, in spiritual dimensions – we are 'born again'.[173] Often a 'gospel call' is given in terms of 'ask Jesus into your life' – for Him to give Himself to me. What we actually need to do, should be to give ourselves to Him! There needs to be an act of recognition and submission to make a start as givers. We are to become 'workers together with Him'.[174] This starts with:

Family Membership. We are born again into new life, moving then from becoming disciples (learners) to incorporation into eternal living and in new dimensions, as we are baptised into the Team. Jesus' commission was to 'make disciples . . . baptising them into the name of the Father and of the Son and of the Holy Spirit';[175] part of what God is and what He is doing. Not just membership, but identity. This then moves on into:

The Family Business. Bringing life to the world. God does not call people just to fill churches on Sundays, He calls us to be agents of heaven in His world, working inside it, where we meet and know real people. In Chapter 3, we saw Paul explore the mind of Jesus – selfless, serving and then sacrificial – even to death. How he used this example to speak to us, to have the same mind; the same mission. As we fulfil this in total self-giving, we become part of the great plan of God. Our minds have become much bigger, indeed, 'we have the mind of Christ'.[176] Amazingly, we can think 'God thoughts'. So we are thus not just agents, but intelligent agents. We start to reflect the Family likeness,

173. John 3:3-6.
174. 2 Corinthians 6:1, NKJV.
175. Matthew 28:19.
176. 1 Corinthians 2:16.

the Family business, Family values and also see the Family results as we move on.

Family growth and development. God, as it were, lives in us as we become not only givers, but blessed givers, living by the direction and dynamic of the Holy Spirit. 'The Spirit of truth . . . lives with you and will be in you'.[177] He does not leave us to just 'muddle along'! We find meaning and fulfilment in renewed living in God's dynamics; not superhuman, but suprahuman – bigger than the ordinary. Sharing in the life and activity of God. We have new powers and abilities through His Holy Spirit within us, just as Jesus had promised: 'you will receive power when the Holy Spirit comes on you; and you will be my witnesses'.[178] Power yes, in terms of ability, but what about the hard work of keeping going? Might I start to run dry, as time goes on? Is that a fear?

Paul experienced a huge range of hardships as he travelled the Mediterranean world. He had been imprisoned, beaten, stoned (and left for dead), shipwrecked, in danger, misrepresented, hungry, sleepless and more (some more than once).[179] As he neared the end of his course, in Rome, he looked back and wrote, 'I have learned to be content whatever the circumstances.'[180] 'Content' does not mean 'stoically taking life's blows on the chin'. It means that he is actually happy and fulfilled in doing it. He goes on to say, 'I have learned the secret of being content . . . I can do all this through him who gives me strength.'[181] These are big words, but not grandiose or unrealistic. They were Paul's

177. John 14:17; 11; 19.
178. Acts 1:8.
179. 2 Corinthians 11:23-27.
180. Philippians 4:11.
181. Philippians 4:12-13.

working reality, statements of fact. In a way it is a secret; outsiders do not understand it, or even believe that it exists. But it is a secret that we can know too – we can be happy and settled in our call to serve. We do not have to be afraid of running dry, or being overcome by circumstances.

We can know God's infinite resources in us – not passively; our giving is the expressing of God's giving. We 'participate in the divine nature'.[182] We do not 'become' God, but we enter into His thinking and purposes for His world, with His resources. What He is overflows into us and through us. We also participate 'in his sufferings'.[183] This is not an expression of the doctrine of Theosis, becoming 'part of God'. We are called to live *agape* like Him and to use His resources, administering them by His motivation – love, and His mentality – generosity. These and so many spiritual parameters are a mystery. God can give 'more than all we ask or imagine'.[184] In praying we explore God's willingness and ability to give to us; even beyond our good desires and most spectacular dreams! We can never outgive Him, so in that sense can always afford to give. Don't be afraid, be amazed – indeed, be amazing! Be a world-changer, like God, with God and for God. God is at work in you, 'to will and to act in order to fulfil his good purpose'.[185] That does not just happen, we need to be 'workers together with Him',[186] positively committed, always involved.

What a transition we see in this chapter – a God who calls us into physical existence and then totally transforms us into working partnership with Him in the world He made and loves.

---

182. 2 Peter 1:4.
183. Philippians 3:10.
184. Ephesians 3:20.
185. Philippians 2:13.
186. 2 Corinthians 6:1, NKJV.

Chapter 13

Challenging the Church

What has gone before has largely been directed at the individual Christian 'giver', or potential giver. It is also true of the Church, which should be a body of givers – Jesus' agents in today's world. The early Church gave itself away in two notable ways:

- **In Jerusalem**, where things started at Pentecost, they met together in the Temple and in their homes – a new development, which would soon change as the Church grew and had new and larger structural and administrative needs. But there were needs – which they met by compassionate giving.[187] This was initially within the Church context, but soon moved outwards.

- **Later in Antioch**, a thriving Church in another country, Syria (where the Church had been stirred to go by persecution), soon expanded beyond Jerusalem and Palestine (the 'go-mentality' was already happening, primed by the persecution following the martyrdom of Stephen).[188] The Holy Spirit now spoke about more going.[189] As a result, Barnabas, their best pastor, and

---

187. Acts 2:44-45.
188. Acts 11:19-20.
189. Acts 13:1-3.

Paul, their best preacher, were sent out. If they gave their best – where did that leave them? We need to remember that God looks after the consequences of our obedience. Mission is Jesus' command. They did it and it changed the Mediterranean world, even to the extent of the initial opening up of Europe. The long-term consequences of Christian living and giving were becoming worldwide . . . The call and mandate from Jesus is about thinking and acting outwards in three ways:

1. Look out. In today's Church, we need to be careful of any mentality which means we look inward, as we struggle to survive and maintain the status quo. We spend ourselves catering for the desires and preferences of our members, instead of investing into our community, our nation and our world. Archbishop William Temple said, 'The Church is the only society that exists for the benefit of those who are not its members',[190] but often we can slip into the disobedience of holding God to ourselves and have often compounded this by neglect of the Great Commission. We are not 'givers' and thus have disqualified ourselves from being 'more blessed'. We can lose our mind for mission and at the same time, the sense of strength, vitality and joy evaporate. Anything resembling miracles in Church life are often at risk of being met by suspicion, unbelief, or disapproval. The same happened after the great events in Acts 3. The religious authorities moved in heavy-handedly, to stop this outburst of life – it was not what 'should have been done' – it broke the 'rules'![191]

---

190. William Temple (1881–1944), www.newworldencyclopedia.org/entry/William_Temple (accessed 15 February 2023).
191. Acts 4:1-3.

Jesus said, 'go and make disciples of all nations',[192] but what does that mean? 'Learners of Jesus'; the starting point of evangelism. The good news of a God who gives forgiveness and new life. Other things go together with this, like pastoral care and helping with 'needs', be they physical, social, material, spiritual, or whatever. These things are not the 'gospel' *per se*. In my opinion, some churches, although doing 'good things', have lost sight of this; the aim should be to see salvation and life. Other things follow.

Losing sight of the vital need of biblical proclamation seems to be commonplace. So, what do we get? Nice people doing nice things, but with no cutting edge may then become critical of churches with a 'message' tend to thrive, while others tend to fade away. Should we be surprised? Other activities do not necessarily indicate life. The Church is not a religious club, or a Social Services' agency.

2. Give out. The principles of financial and resource-giving goes back to Old Testament times. The community of Israel had twelve tribes. Eleven of them 'gave', to support the ministry tribe – that is, the Levites. Giving by God's people, for God's people, doing God's work. It needs realistic resourcing. God gives at all levels, starting with life; so should we. Giving 'in kind' (things and agricultural produce) is not so relevant in the culture of most of us today, as we deal in money. Giving, however, is still important for the same reason (as well as many others). The function of the Church – its staff, facilities and ministries need money. Giving into local ministry should be one of the keys to successful wider ministry – often called 'mission', but not always just in terms of 'evangelism'.

---

192. Matthew 28:19.

The subject of money is always potentially divisive. We get very defensive and self-justifying, but it is an important enabling resource. We need to see this in two ways:

- **Personal giving.** Biblically, this can be seen as tithes and offerings, which we have already spoken about in this book. Tithes are proportional to income − traditionally 10 per cent, but it is not about a mathematical game of self-justification. In theory, nobody gets nothing, though some people are not far off that, but circumstances can change for anybody, by losing a job, illness, unexpected new commitments, or whatever. They will make prayerful re-thinking necessary. Our giving needs to be realistic and imaginative. 'Offerings' are over and above; special responses to the goodness of God in unexpected needs. Often, we simply do not take the time to stop and think how good He has been and what we could, or should do to express our gratitude. There is an important wider spectrum of giving, too, to which we need to have a personal input and responsibility . . .

- **Church giving.** Does your church tithe itself? Giving away money into 'outside' causes, proportional to its own income? Also giving resources into the local community, or further afield? This is an important part of local responsibility and indirect mission. My own church has been doing this for many years, starting at 12 per cent, and has slowly increased it. We have not been losers as a result. The church has grown and three times has had to face the problem of how to handle too many people for our building. God is no man's debtor.[193]

---

193. See Matthew 20:1-16.

Giving is about more than just money. It is also about personal giving – what you are and what you have. That includes your gifting, both natural and spiritual (though these will often overlap). They are all part of the resources for the full functioning of the Church. We have already addressed abilities which can be 'tithed' in a sense, but let us just consider two important ones here. Time (of which we never seem to have enough) – it is amazing what good time-management can achieve; and mobility, which is also related to time and money; the practicality of going, short or longer-term to somewhere else, as God prompts.

How might the Church give out? Let me give you two examples of giving into the local community. I will start with car parking – always a hot issue! We do not have enough on our site for our normal use on Sundays, but this is not usually a problem. There is more available to share with local shop use. If we have a big event on a weekday, all the local spaces are under great pressure. A few years ago, the shopkeepers came out as a deputation. There was no space left for their customers (that means 'money', a serious issue!). In principle all local street-parking is for local use, but they had a point. What should we do? Ignore them? No, that would be irresponsible for us as a community member, so we called a meeting with the shopkeepers and the local borough councillor. We all agreed that there was not enough local parking. Clearly the council needed to make more space – which they did; but the existing space had no marked bays, so what was already available was being inefficiently used. The church said, 'We will pay for the marking.' The shopkeepers were amazed! There was still not enough space for high-demand times, so we made arrangements with another nearby church to use their space and also with the local pub. And whenever we have a big event, we provide 'no parking' notices and parking attendants from our membership. Problem solved; community happy; low-key evangelism active. Many church members are starting to offer themselves in the local community. There is a local food bank, a furniture storehouse and a practical help group. There has also been overseas activity, which has included whole families, even their children, going to such places as France, Russia, Uganda, India, the Gambia and Romania, to help with short-term projects. They return as 'different people' – their giving has changed their lives. It has changed the church too. We are thinking differently. Everybody wins!

Another issue was raised some years ago – the effective use of our building. Many churches stand almost empty for most of the week. Their physical design (often from practices many years ago) may be rather limiting to current usefulness. When we were looking to expand considerably our own facilities, we were stimulated to think, not only for our own growth-needs, but also for the needs of the wider Christian community. This could be in terms of the local Church community, as well as regional and national resourcing.

The building has become a very popular conference centre and can offer a wide range of facilities – including catering and toilets! The latter are often a very inadequate and unwelcoming feature of many church buildings – 'by their loos you shall know them'! We are very happy to support local government, health and education events, as well as (obviously) 'Christian' ones. It has done us no harm. Indeed, we are privileged to be able to share ourselves and our resources.

God gives to needs at all levels, starting with life; so should we. That needs to be realistic. When talking about giving money, Paul wrote in 2 Corinthians 9:7 that 'God loves a cheerful [Greek word: 'hilarious'] giver'.[7] Is your giving (of whatever) an enjoyable experience? It is not about 'Oh dear, here comes the plate (bag)', but 'Where is it? I am ready to give'.

That is about 'my church'. What about the 'local Church'? Churches are usually not alone; there are others of different denominations, with different ways of doing things. We may disagree with some of them, but if they are living out the gospel, they are part of God's work in the locality. The two key points of agreement needed are defined for us by Paul in 1 Corinthians 15:3-4: 'Christ died for our sins . . . [and] was raised on the third day . . .' If we agree on those, we can work together. The public at large use our differences to criticise and to snipe at us (often justifiably) and to excuse their non-participation. If we show genuine commitment to each other and our community, attitudes and opportunities change.

This started in our own (county) town about forty-five years ago, with a central monthly Sunday evening event for youth. By 1981, thirty-five churches had agreed to have a year of mission together in three localities, finishing with a week in the largest hall in town. It happened the following year and concluded with 1,000 people attending. Publicity, rentals and the costs of the visiting team from York for the final week were all covered. This was subsequently repeated twice. There are now regular events together, particularly at Easter in the town square and at the castle. 'Street Pastors'[194] has been functioning for ten years now and

---

194. www.streetpastors.org/ (accessed 15 February 2023).

youth work in schools is growing fast. The local authorities have been impressed and are now asking for help with our expertise.

We are living in a time of favour that would have been unimaginable before. It started by giving ourselves to each other.

3. Go out. Much of the overseas mission in the last 200 years has been done through missionary societies, rather than through the local Church itself, with some notable exceptions. Letting somebody else do the organising, recruiting, training, fundraising and support has been done by external agencies, though some churches gave support through these. The 'call' of missionaries often came through outside events, not specifically aimed internal preaching programmes. There had been little 'mission mentality' in many church members. In smaller churches, the use of external agencies is understandable, but as mission is meant to start on the doorstep – 'Jerusalem . . . to the end of the earth',[195] that may be a reason why some churches stay small, shrink, or even disappear.

The New Testament Church actively 'called' and 'sent out', as the Holy Spirit led them. We need to rediscover this mentality of giving our best. As we see in Acts 11:19-30, Antioch was a classic example of this. Beginning mission 'at home' ('Jerusalem') is an important starting point. It requires recognition, commitment and involvement by the church membership. The not-infrequent attitude of the Church over the centuries has been 'the minister does everything', that is why we pay him! This is totally unbiblical. 'You are the body of Christ, and each one of

---

195. Acts 1:8.

you is a part of it'[196] is about involvement, responsibility and use of gifting by all. The historical rise of 'priestcraft' to a position of power and exclusivity has virtually destroyed right functioning in some churches. It should be about committed giving by all – the Transforming Principle in all expressions of Church function – children's and youth work, home groups, provision for the elderly and also all the practicalities of the use of premises, music, technology and any other valid ministry. We often uninspiringly call them 'volunteers'! They are all workers together – valuable, indeed, vital. Effective wider mission stands on the foundation of a stable local Church. That should then become the resource for mission outwards.

Mission was Jesus' mandate for the Church as a whole, as we read in Matthew 28:19 – 'Therefore go and make disciples of all nations'. This was not an option for those who felt like it, or those who could cope, or those who had a guilt complex for not doing it. The prelude to Pentecost was a reinforcement of this command, '. . . you will receive power when the Holy Spirit comes on you; and you will be my witnesses . . . to the ends of the earth'.[197] Not to do so is disobedience; it is also to lose the validity of being a church – no longer living out the reality of the body of Christ and the Great Commission of Jesus.

Looking, giving and going are the right thought pattern that all Christians individually and together need to have not just in their Vision Statement, but at the front of their minds and activity. Is this why many churches just 'fade away'?

Finally, we need to beware of rigidly trying to get things 'right' as a church. Control can be the touch of death! Be

196. 1 Corinthians 12:27.
197. Acts 1:8.

amazed at seeing God at work as we learn to relax and give, not lapsing

into sitting back with a sigh of self-satisfaction, while everything quietly collapses! We can be de-transformed by default!

Chapter 14

Where Does it End?

Being a giver, as an individual, a family, or a church may look like a one-way, never-ending nightmare! But *blessed* giving will never be that. If our giving is in biblical dimensions, it is God's way and He does not do nightmares! He is a God of delight.

Does it end when Jesus returns? We often look to this as a stimulus or a warning to examine what we are doing and why. We do not want to be embarrassed by being caught in inactivity or sin. A coming Jesus challenges the uncertainty of human 'certainty'. We have no idea of precisely when that will be, in spite of many attempts to untangle the accounts of the Last Times over the centuries (to this day). Were we to know, the temptation may be to set our clocks for the big Day, then sit back and enjoy ourselves in the interim. No pressures to be givers of anything. Then . . . the Rapture and off to heaven! But what might that mean? Is it some great holiday resort in the sky, with harps and angels? No, even there we will be givers in worship as we are called to be here and now. Worship is giving and giving is worship. They both express our positive relationship with God. They are both eternally relevant. They are actually supposed to be normalities, but in the now, they are sometimes felt as supranormal – are they something to strive for, or maybe to think of as a little odd? Is it OK not to achieve them?

So, whatever the 'future' holds long-term (and that will indeed be wonderful and beyond all our speculation) we are not called by God to live in the future now; it does not exist yet – in a sense, it never will. It will become the new present! That is the time-dimension to which we are always called, the ongoing 'now' which we already have. 'Blessed giving' is always and eternally relevant.

God's call to each and all of us is to look outwards continually, to see the opportunities that could involve us and the whole range of our resources and then to live out 'giving', whatever that means at the time, with our motives open before God:

- **Unembarrassed** and without any sense of inadequacy or guilt. He does not ask for what do not have; he is totally realistic. And at the end of the day we say, 'We are unworthy servants';[198] would God that I had been able to do more.

- **No 'airs'.** Pride disguised as false modesty – 'Haven't we/I done well?' ... 'God ought to be pleased'! No, we can actually afford to relax, release and be real.

- **No superiority.** 'Well, I have done better than him/her.' As Paul reminded his readers, 'Who are you to judge someone else's servant?'[199] We are called to obey, not to criticise.

- **No 'Lady Bountiful' attitudes.** The 'impressive' benefactress, who builds her image by self-justifying giving. It may not actually be generosity; she probably has plenty more. Note that this can also be applied to

198. Luke 17:10.
199. Romans 14:4.

'he'! There has been no sacrifice. This was typified by the rich at the Temple, as we read in Mark 12:41-42. Their 'generous' giving was a religious performance. It had not stretched them or their thinking – unlike the quiet widow.

- **Just pure reality in humble joy.** 'Cheerful givers'[200] who do it because they want to; they are looking to and loving, to pour themselves out to bless other people and to glorify God, and to love doing it.

The gospel *is* about pure and complete reality, life 'to the full';[201] it impacts on everything we are and do; our attitudes and actions, work and leisure, Sundays and weekdays. We are always 'on duty', but never thinking of duty as onerous. Life is for receiving and sharing, it always has been. It is not a right, it is a privileged gift. 'Sharing' should mean enjoying together what is often called 'fellowship'. The Greek word is *koinonia*, which can also be translated as partnership, or participation – we are in it together. Interaction with other Christians in worship, relaxation, learning and in specific events – together in Christ, members of His body; doing life together and stimulating mutual discovery, growth and enjoyment. But our sharing must not be cliquey. It should also mean giving the entry and experience of these things to people at present outside the Faith, to stimulate them to look at the paucity of even the 'good things' in their own lives and to reach out into the generosity of God's grace. Call it 'evangelism' if you like; somebody probably did it for you once! It is about givers looking to generate new givers, as they come to faith. It always has been; the

---

200. See 2 Corinthians 9:7.
201. John 10:10.

ongoing repetition of the Great Commission: 'Go and make disciples . . . teaching them to obey everything I have commanded you.'[202]

Sadly, Christians have often been very unattractive! Who or what has put you off in the past? Can you look at your own way of living and say, 'Have I ever put anyone off?' But attractive living can fall into the trap of being little more than amusement. Being outgoing means more than just getting people involved in Christian activities (which can sometimes actually be rather dull). Those activities should both directly and indirectly 'say something'. We are not called to feed the fish, but to catch them! What attracted me as a teenager was the great fun these people had together (some of it almost outrageous) and also the inclusion and integration of biblical teaching in what they said and did – even the fun. It was a stimulating and disarming package and I wanted it!

Who passed on the Good News to you? When? How? Thank God. And have you thanked them? Is it too late? If not, a letter, phone call, email or a visit is in order. Who have you passed it on to? Have you started? Are you still doing it? It is an ongoing privilege for every Christian. It does not finish until life does.

Our giving expresses our living. It should be attractive and also informative and challenging, always unconsciously on display; demonstrating the reality of what God can do in real people. It should never stop. Rather like the card game of Bridge, we should play 'Open Misère' with our cards visible on the table, from a position of security, knowing that we can win the trick. We should be open and honest, disarmingly so, willing to risk ourselves for the benefit of

---

202. Matthew 28:19-20.

the other person. Knowing that whatever problems may be visible in our lives at present, we are actually becoming winners. In some parts of the world, even today, we hear of persecution, murders, burning of churches. Even in 'civilised' Europe, Christians are treated as naïve and detached from reality. We are unfairly criticised, made the butt of jokes (some of them very unfunny), made to look stupid, taken advantage of . . . But the final message of the book of Revelation is 'we win'.

humanity wins, no matter what apparent disasters may happen in the meantime. History has been full of them!

Being a Christian more than in name has always been made difficult by an unbelieving world. That is particularly so for teenagers, who are wanting to do the right thing, but have limited ability and experience to try to achieve it. They are very aware of their physical and emotional insecurity. They are still learning the basics of the Faith, let alone the strengths of apologetics. Many of these things will change and develop as their education and understanding progress, but it is important for us as the Church to see that they are spiritually educated as well, and to support them with encouragement in their difficulties. Do they see us as allies, or critics? They also need to be trained to be givers and given the opportunity and respect to learn by experience (even allowed the space to get things wrong!). In all these things, we are playing for the long-term victory, but even in the challenges of the present there are often encouragements, sometimes in very unexpected ways. God knows that we need a lift every so often. Time and again, we turn out to be the overwhelming minority – to the delight and surprise of all!

So, where does it end? The simple answer is, it doesn't! The 'I am' God always 'is'. So the God who is love always is. Christian giving is the way of life for all of time (and eternity). It always has been. There is nothing new here, why should there be? Look at the cross. Jesus is the greatest Giver and it is our turn at present, as we look to Jesus, the God who is love and who spares nothing to rescue a lost world, who does not actually see that they even have a problem! They are much more interested in money, position, self-expression and in 'security' – which does not actually exist in their parameters of living. Indeed, it cannot!

The ministry of 'God in Christ Jesus' is still being carried out through each generation of givers. We look at Jesus, who 'for the joy that was set before him . . . endured the cross, scorning its shame. . .'[203] He could see the outcome of His sacrifice, so can we. Giving is not about being miserable losers! Christian giving is also the way of life for eternity. It is a practical expression of worship.

So, back to the beginning – the Transforming Principle that we read in Acts 20:35: 'It is more blessed to give than to receive.' When receiving becomes an end in itself – the philosophy of a 'getting' world – it has no blessing attached. It has already had its 'reward'[204] and is often disappointed. There is nothing else left to have and at death, hope dies too. End of story? There is also the matter of judgement!

Conversely, when giving is the aim, it releases us from the world of selfishness into the discovering and enacting the thinking and living of God Himself; partners in rescuing a dying world, indeed, in being part of delivering the rescue package. As we do that, we are also blessed – in receiving! We are given the resources to make it possible, the desire

---

203. Hebrews 12:2.
204. Matthew 6:2.

to deploy them and the thrill of seeing God's purposes being worked out. Two-way blessing in giving – and also in receiving – is God's stamp of approval. It is not our aim or desire (that would kill it immediately); it comes as a delightful surprise!

'It is more blessed to give than to receive'; do you believe that? It is the way that God works, the way that Jesus taught and the way that history has shown to be right. Aim at giving and the receiving will look after itself. It is the only way that works. Can you add yourself to the list of witnesses? At the end of the day, while we as servants are unworthy, Jesus says to us, 'Enter into the joy of your Lord, good and faithful servant.'[205]

So let us learn how to serve
And in our lives enthrone Him
Each other's needs to prefer
For it is Christ we're serving'.
This is our God, the Servant King,
He calls us now to follow Him
To give our lives as a daily offering
Of worship to the Servant King.[206]

Is the Transforming Principle upside down? No! The rest of the world is the 'wrong way up' – their priorities can never deliver an ultimately worthwhile purpose, fulfilment and eternal satisfaction. Selfishness is the basis of sin, and the outcome of sin is disintegration and death. God offers life through the unlikely pathway of death – He pays off the consequences of sin and opens up a totally new way

205. Matthew 25:21, NKJV.
206. 'The Servant King', Graham Kendrick Copyright © 1983 Thankyou Music.

of living. We enter that life also through 'death' – to our old priorities, motives and values. The new life continues through as a succession of 'deaths', releasing ourselves and our resources in apparent 'loss', while actually receiving infinite gains. 'He is no fool who gives what he cannot keep to gain what he cannot lose.'[207] Apparent 'onerous duty' will disappear in pleasurable delight, because it can see the end, as Jesus did. The end is worth it, regardless of the cost. It is all about 'the upward call of God in Christ'.[208]

So, who or what is 'transformed' as we work out the Transforming Principle? If we opt in, it can be anybody and everything. 'Blessedness' is especially for the givers. They enter into new dimensions of relationship and function with God Himself. That is not so much a 'reward' but a living reality, a natural outcome – receiving, almost without realising it! It is not an aim in itself, or it would not be 'blessed'! Those who seek 'blessing' for itself, with apparently 'good' motives, may well not find it. They will have the heartache, but end up in frustration. Our first steps into the life of faith are in reaching out to God in repentance and then moving into receiving His grace. With that, we can then start to become givers . . .

Even as 'more experienced' Christians, we still need to be receivers. God is the great Giver of everything and it would be foolish to refuse Him. We never grow out of our dependence on Him. 'Blessedness' is relative – 'It is *more* blessed to give' – but if our receiving is from God we are, by definition, 'blessed' already! The challenge of the Transforming Principle is that we recognise the call of God to deploy what we have received to bless others. The

---

207. Jim Elliot, www.brainyquote.com/quotes/jim_elliot_189244 (accessed 15 February 2023).
208. Philippians 3:14, NKJV.

depth of our spirituality will be defined by the expression of entering into the thinking and action of God. So, 'Where does it end?' It doesn't!

Pray 'What does that require of me now?' today. Then start where you can see . . . and keep going! 'Enter into the joy of your lord',[209] the great Giver. 'Be steadfast, immovable, always abounding in the work of the Lord, knowing that your labour is not in vain in the Lord.'[210] *You are not wasting your time.*

209. Matthew 25:21, NKJV.
210. 1 Corinthians 15:58, NKJV.

Chapter 15

In Conclusion

Letting go of any 'security' is always disturbing, even when done in a deliberate or planned way. When it involves actual 'giving', we need to think in terms of what is being given, to whom and why. Sometimes the perceived need is (almost mathematically) clear, particularly when money is involved; it may be more open-ended. When there is a possibility of a continuing and possibly increasing call on our resources, there may be a developing feeling of 'sacrifice'. This moves us from the concept of discomfort to that of threat! This may not have been evident at the beginning. How should we react to this, particularly as Christians?

A vital part of our thinking and way of life should always be to live out a continually developing relationship with our God, usually expressed in such activities as praying and Bible-reading – two basic Christian disciplines. These are not exclusive to other ways of relating and living and will include our thinking on giving – moving from the feelings of rigidity in 'have to' to progressive release into 'ought to', 'need to', 'want to', into 'delight to'! All the way, we will have been increasing in our practical understanding and love of God. It pleases Him too!

'*God is love.*'[211] He is always the great outgoing Giver, on whom we are totally dependent for 'life and breath and

---

211. 1 John 4:8.

everything',[212] ultimately in giving Himself – 'he loved us and sent his Son as propitiation for our sins'.[213] As a result of this, we start to live a life of love too. Jesus commands His followers 'love each other as I have loved you'[214] and then goes on to say 'nobody has greater love that this, that he lays down his life for his friends – and *you* are *my* friends'.[215] Love was the hallmark of the early Church and people commented, 'How [these Christians] love one another'![216] This lifestyle is still a major challenge to a selfish world. It speaks into reality; it is not just words.

So, God is love personified and the essence of love is that it gives and loves to give. Perfect love gives perfectly – without limit and for as much and as long as needed. This is the life-dimension to which we are called – to be like God! He understands giving more than anybody. He has been demonstrating it from the beginning of time. He gives it in terms of total relevance to every situation in human experience. Ultimately, 'God so loved the world that he gave his one and only Son'.[217] No limits! The great Lover is the great Giver. He understands sacrifice more than anybody and, as He calls us into new life through Jesus, He calls us into new living. This is giving a dynamic relevance into all the dimensions of who we are. To what extent? Jesus said, 'I am the good shepherd . . . [who] lays down his life for the sheep.'[218] As partakers of His love and His life, the great Lover calls us into the family business – extending that love ourselves to whoever needs it!

212. Acts 17:25.
213. 1 John 4:10.
214. John 15:12.
215. See John 15:13-14.
216. Tertullian, www.oxfordreference.com/display/10.1093/acref/9780191843730.001.00 01/q-oro-ed5-00010813;jsessionid=E78EA209BB2A64AE8E460BE31BD15E5B#:~:text='Look%2C'%20they%20say%2C,readier%20to%20kill%20each%20other) (accessed 6 March 2023).
217. John 3:16.
218. John 10:11.

Love cannot exist in a vacuum; it needs to burst out and express itself. Its overwhelming desire is to become living reality and to give outwards. It desires and hopes to be reciprocated, but can persist even though it may be disappointed. Love 'always protects . . . trusts . . . hopes . . . perseveres. Love never fails'.[219] It is the driving force of the Transforming Principle; the outgoing action that demonstrates that *'It is more blessed to give than to receive'*. The practicalities of the 'giving' are part of Christian living and living Christianity.

We become aware of the needs in the course of living in a world littered with problems. God may point to some of them as a consequence of our praying, reading, hearing and seeing what is happening. These bring us closer to Him and His world; we enter into a new and exciting dimension – 'we have the mind of Christ'[220] – we start thinking God-thoughts and God-perceptions! These then prompt us to explore God-actions; doing what He would do. That may even be expressed in miracles, when appropriate.

So what has God been saying (or trying to say) to you? How is it that you can become increasingly part of what He is doing in His world? Through the centuries, that has meant His people stepping out into imaginative giving, directed by His Holy Spirit to provide for opportunities from what resources they have. None of us has 'nothing'; our biggest resource is ourselves – what God has made us; the temptation is to think only in terms of money.

Our motivation is often inversely proportional to our wealth. In Mark 12:41-44 Jesus criticised some 'big givers' for putting on a show and commended a poor widow.

---

219. 1 Corinthians 13:7-8.
220. 1 Corinthians 2:16.

Paul commended the Macedonian Christians – 'In the midst of a very severe trial, their overflowing joy and their extreme poverty welled up in rich generosity . . . they gave as much as they were able, and even beyond their ability. [221] His observation was 'whoever sows sparingly will also reap sparingly, and whoever sows generously will also reap generously.'[222] Are you afraid of stepping out of your generosity comfort zone? God looks after the consequences of our obedience, 'so that in all things at all times . . . you will abound in every good work.'[223] Jesus said 'seek first [the kingdom of God] and his righteousness . . .'[224] everything else follows.

What has been your experience as a giver? Where are you being challenged? What will you do? I have found a helpful way forward is to pray, 'Lord, show me what you want . . . and I will do it.' When God speaks, the only appropriate response is 'yes'! Risky? Maybe, but honest. Are you ready for surprises? They will be good: 'Enter into the joy of your lord'![225]

221. 2 Corinthians 8:2-3.
222. 2 Corinthians 9:6.
223. 2 Corinthians 9:8.
224. Matthew 6:33.
225. Matthew 25:21.

130

Epilogue

God is good. Amazingly good – in every way. All the good things we are and have come from Him: 'No good thing does he withhold from those whose way of life is blameless',[226] though He does that in His own way. His love is totally practical – it fits our real needs in all aspects of life – body, soul and spirit; it leads into 'life . . . to the full'[227] ultimately through giving Himself in Jesus on the cross, to restore us to Himself and to give us the honour of being part of all He is doing in our world: 'Oh, the depth of the riches and wisdom . . . of God! . . . Who has ever given to God, that God should repay . . . from him and through him and for him are all things.'[228]

How should I respond to all this? 'Offer your [body] as a living sacrifice . . . this is . . . true and proper worship.'[229] The only realistic 'thank you' and the start of a giving mentality, releasing all I am and have into His service. This may look like a huge threat, but 'It is more blessed to give . . .' So, 'What shall I return to [Him] for all his goodness to me?' I will take the salvation that He gives, pray to Him, and fulfil all my promises to Him.

---

226. Psalm 84:11.
227. John 10:10.
228. Romans 11:33-36.
229. Romans 12:1.

Oh Thou who camest from above
The pure celestial fire to impart,
Kindle a flame of sacred love
On the mean altar of my heart!

There let it for thy glory burn
With inextinguishable blaze,
And trembling to its source return
In humble prayer and fervent praise

Jesus, confirm my heart's desire,
To work, and speak, and think for thee;
Still let me guard the holy fire,
And still stir up thy gift in me.

Ready for all thy perfect will,
My acts of faith and love repeat;
Till death thy endless mercies seal,
And make the sacrifice complete.

(Charles Wesley, 1707-88)[230]

This is living! It is for all of life! It is totally consuming. It comes to an even more amazing (non!)-conclusion!

---

230. https://hymnary.org/text/o_thou_who_camest_from_above (accessed 6 March 2023).